AS/A-LEVEL YEAR 1
STUDENT GUIDE

WJEC/Eduqas

Geography

Changing places

David Burtenshaw

HODDER
EDUCATION
AN HACHETTE UK COMPANY

For Amelie, Matteo, Alessandro, Noah, Matilda and Maisie, twenty first-century citizens.

Hodder Education, an Hachette UK company, Blenheim Court, George Street, Banbury, Oxfordshire OX16 5BH

Orders

Bookpoint Ltd, 130 Park Drive, Milton Park, Abingdon, Oxfordshire OX14 4SB

tel: 01235 827827

fax: 01235 400401

e-mail: education@bookpoint.co.uk

Lines are open 9.00 a.m.–5.00 p.m., Monday to Saturday, with a 24-hour message answering service. You can also order through the Hodder Education website: www.hoddereducation.co.uk

© David Burtenshaw 2016

ISBN 978-1-4718-6405-6

First printed 2016

Impression number 5 4 3 2 1

Year 2020 2019 2018 2017 2016

Cover photograph: dabldy/Fotolia. Other photographs: David Burtenshaw (p. 16); akoppo1/Fotolia (p. 18); Jack Sullivan and Paul White – North West England/Alamy Stock Photo (p. 27); David Bagnall/Alamy Stock Photo (p. 68); A.P.S. (UK)/Alamy Stock Photo (p. 98)

This Guide has been written specifically to support students preparing for the WJEC/Eduqas AS and A-level Geography examinations. The content has been neither approved nor endorsed by WJEC/Eduqas and remains the sole responsibility of the author.

Typeset by Integra Software Services Pvt. Ltd., Pondicherry, India

Printed in Italy

Contents

Content Guidance

Questions & Answers

Getting the most from this book

Exam tips

Advice on key points in the text to help you learn and recall content, avoid pitfalls, and polish your exam technique in order to boost your grade.

Knowledge check

Rapid-fire questions throughout the Content Guidance section to check your understanding.

Knowledge check answers

1 Turn to the back of the book for the Knowledge check answers.

Summaries

■ Each core topic is rounded off by a bullet-list summary for quick-check reference of what you need to know.

Commentary on the questions

Tips on what you need to do to gain full marks, indicated by the icon ⓔ

Exam-style questions

Sample student answers

Practise the questions, then look at the student answers that follow.

Commentary on sample student answers

Read the comments (preceded by the icon ⓔ) showing how many marks each answer would be awarded in the exam and exactly where marks are gained or lost.

The answer shows that the student has made good use of their home place and has contrasted it with other places within the essay. Knowledge is good and backed up by statistics that must have come from either fieldwork or secondary sources. AO1 is worth 7 marks, because there is little else that could be achieved in the time.

Applies AO2.1c to assess the relative impacts, both positive and negative on groups of people.

There is a statement in the conclusion that tries to assess the overall impact. Likewise the first sentence of the third paragraph is trying to provide assessment. Perhaps more assessment could have been used as the essay went along. Is there enough about people who are mentioned but only as broad categories? Nevertheless, this is a top band response worth 5 marks.

This question relied on a good essay, which makes up for weaker understanding of the data.

ⓔ **Total score: 14/16 marks awarded**

Question 4

ⓔ This question follows the format for the Eduqas A-level extended response question, which will be questions 11 and 12 in the actual examination. You have 20 minutes to read the question, plan and write the essay.

To what extent are rural settlements no longer villages, hamlets and farms serving a rural economy? [15 marks]

To what extent are rural settlements no longer villages, hamlets and farms serving a rural economy?	AO1	AO2.1a	AO2.1b	AO2.1c	AO3.1	AO3.2	Total
	10			5			15

Student A

Villages are changing because of counter-urbanisation, which is the movement of people from towns to villages.

People want to live in the countryside because it is more pleasant than living in congested towns, which have higher crime, more pollution and less open space. So people move to villages where the environment is less polluted and more pleasant. Many of these people move just before retirement or continue to commute back to the town where they work.

People no longer work in agriculture or fishing because of the EU quotas and because of mechanisation of farming. Many farms now offer tourist accommodation and some have other activities such as a farm shop. Barns have been sold off for offices or for housing conversions.

Changing places 109

■ About this book

Much of the knowledge and understanding needed for AS and A-level Geography builds on what you have learned for GCSE Geography, but with an added focus on geographical skills and techniques, and concepts. This guide has been designed to help you succeed in the Eduqas and WJEC Geography AS and A-level **Changing places**. The topics covered in this guide are:

- **Section B of A-level Eduqas Component 1:** Changing landscapes and Changing places
- **Section A of AS Eduqas Component 2:** Changing places
- **Unit 2 of WJEC AS:** Changing places

The format of the different examination papers is summarised in the table below.

Specification and paper number	Total time for Changing places	Total marks for Changing places	Structured questions	Extended response/ essay	Fieldwork
Eduqas A-level Component 1	**50 min** in paper lasting 1h 45 min	41/82	Section B has TWO compulsory, structured questions with data-response marked out of 13	Section B has ONE from a choice of two marked out of 15	No questions, but can be used to support your responses
Eduqas AS Component 2	**40 min** in paper lasting 1h 15 min	40/80	Section A has TWO compulsory, structured questions with data-response worth 7–10	Included as the final part of the two questions marked out of either 10 or 13	Section B has THREE compulsory questions including ONE on your own investigation marked out of 40
WJEC AS Unit 2	**37 min** in paper lasting 1h 30 min	32/80	Section A has TWO compulsory structured questions with data-response marked out of 16	None	Section B has THREE compulsory questions including ONE on your own fieldwork marked out of 32

The guide has the following main objectives:

- It provides you with key concepts, definitions, theories and examples that may be used to answer questions in the examination. The examples have been designed to provide you with alternatives to your home area wherever possible.
- It provides potential fieldwork investigation topics that you may follow up either as a part of the fieldwork requirement for Changing places or for further development when you are considering the topic for the A-level Independent Investigation.
- It will suggest self-study tasks and further reading that will enhance your knowledge and understanding before you enter the examinations.
- Finally, it will give you the opportunity to test yourself through Knowledge check questions, which are designed to help you to check your depth of knowledge. You will also benefit from noting the Exam tips, which provide further help in determining how to learn key aspects of the course.

The section order follows the Eduqas specification.

The examinations

Eduqas

At **A-level**, the total examination time of Component 1: Changing landscapes and Changing places is 1 hour and 45 minutes. Therefore, you have approximately 50 minutes to answer the three questions in **Section B: Changing places**, which comprises **two** compulsory structured questions that have a gradation of difficulty and **one** extended essay question.

The **structured questions** (Part A) will start with a resource-based question (a), although it might begin with a request for a definition. The resource can lead to a question requiring basic calculation and interpretation of the data, which might be in cartographic, graphical, statistical or photographic form (including air and satellite images). There could also be a short passage of text. The following part will develop from the topic in (a) and will initially require brief description or examination of a relatively small section of the specification. It is worth 13 marks. The **extended response question** (Part B) is a **mini-essay** worth 15 marks, for which you will be expected to offer a more reasoned response in continuous prose. There will be a choice from two titles.

At **AS**, the total examination time of Component 2: Changing places is 1 hour and 15 minutes and you have approximately 40 minutes to answer the two questions in **Section A: Changing places**. The questions will be presented in an answer book where the number of lines beneath each question gives a clue to the level of detail required. Part A in each question is structured and worth 7–10 marks and Part B is a **mini-essay** worth 10–13 marks, depending on the question balance. You will be expected to offer a concise, reasoned response in continuous prose. This guide does not cover the fieldwork questions (**Section B**) at AS, but it will give you suggestions for field investigations.

WJEC

The coverage of Changing places varies in the WJEC specification. This is noted at the start of each section in this guide.

The total examination time of WJEC **AS Unit 2: Changing places** is 1 hour and 30 minutes, in which time you have to answer **two** compulsory structured questions (Section A) and a third question on Physical and/or Human geography fieldwork that you have undertaken (Section B). This guide does not cover the fieldwork question, but it will give you suggestions for field investigations or topics for the NEA Independent Investigation.

The paper format for WJEC is identical to Eduqas, with a gradation of difficulty. The first **two** questions in **Section A** are at AS standard and are answered in an answer booklet. **Section B** tests your fieldwork investigation in Human and Physical Geography, and will examine your ability to demonstrate your knowledge and understanding of the enquiry process as applied to your fieldwork together with an appreciation and understanding of the skills that support your enquiry and its findings.

Timing

The table below shows how to allocate your time depending on the marks to be gained. It can be thought of as '1 mark a minute'.

Mark allocation	Minutes to read, recall and plan	Minutes to write answer
	Read all questions. Decide on order of questions to be answered.	<3
2	1	1
3	1	2
4	1	3
5	1	4
6	1	5
7	1	6
8	2	6
9	2	7
10	2	8
13	2	11
15	2	13

Exam tip

When reading questions, highlight the **command words** and **subject matter** using different colours so that your recall and planning is focused on the question set.

How answers are marked

When your work is marked the examiner will be using **Assessment Objectives (AOs)**. The AOs for both A-level and AS (Eduqas and WJEC) are as follows:

AO1: demonstrate knowledge and understanding of places, environments, concepts, processes, interactions and change at a variety of scales.

AO2: apply knowledge and understanding in different contexts to interpret, analyse and evaluate geographical information and issues:
- **AO2.1a:** apply knowledge and understanding in different contexts to analyse geographical information and issues.
- **AO2.1b:** apply knowledge and understanding in different contexts to interpret geographical information and issues.
- **AO2.1c:** apply knowledge and understanding in different contexts to appraise/judge geographical information.

AO3: use a variety of relevant quantitative, qualitative and fieldwork skills:
- **AO3.1:** investigate geographical questions and issues.
- **AO3.2:** interpret, analyse and evaluate data and evidence.
- **AO3.3:** construct arguments and draw conclusions.

Mark bands

For AOs being tested in each question the marker will make use of mark bands for each AO to guide his/her decision. Here are the qualities that markers will be looking for in each final band.

Band 3 structured questions: answers to the structured questions (/13) will be clear, factually accurate, displaying good knowledge and understanding supported by developed examples, sketches and diagrams. Descriptions will be clear. Statistical work will be complete and understood. Answers to the **mini-essays** (/15) will be well written and argued so that the command word (e.g. explain or evaluate) has been followed. Knowledge will be very detailed, accurate and well supported by examples, and issues will be fully understood.

Band 2 structured questions: answers are often unbalanced and partial responses may be unstructured and make points in a random order. Knowledge is present but not always actually accurate or completely understood. The **mini-essays** will demonstrate some understanding but not all of the points. Examples will be mostly accurate but rather sketchy. Diagrams and statistical work may be less complete. The command word is reinterpreted to mean description rather than discussion or analysis because the answer may take the form of 'all I know that might be relevant'. The coverage might be limited to, for example, two cases when more might gain more credit.

Band 1 structured questions: Answers have very limited and possibly fragmented factual knowledge. There might be no valid examples or just a single example named but not developed. Any diagrams will be basic and/or incomplete. Statistical responses will be neglected. **Mini-essays** may be a set of unrelated, undeveloped ideas, possibly only in note form, and rather hit and miss in their relevance to the question. The command word might be ignored.

0: The response is not credit-worthy because it does not answer the question.

The mini-essays have to be answered in 13–15 minutes, but this does not mean that they should be answered in less depth than the longer essays that are demanded in Component 3. It is a top-notch skill to be able to write concisely including all the relevant detailed arguments and examples in a short space (one side of A4 in 13–15 minutes).

Geographical skills

You are expected to develop various skills as a geographer. Skills are both quantitative, using mathematical, computational and statistical procedures to record phenomena and processes, and qualitative, using non-numerical techniques such as cartographic and GIS data, visual images, and interviewing and oral histories. The specification provides a full list. Some statistical skills have been introduced in this text and others will appear in the companion volumes. The mathematical and statistical tests are not unique to Changing places and are expected to be used and tested where appropriate.

Specialised concepts

The following terms are essential for a twenty-first-century A-level geographer to know and understand. Use them correctly in context whenever you can, because the examination questions will expect you to understand what they mean. This book will highlight where the terms are relevant. (Here they are in alphabetical order.)

Adaptation: the ability to respond to changing events and to reduce current and future vulnerability to change.

Attachment: the linkages between individuals and groups and places.

Causality: the relationship between cause and effect. Everything has a cause or causes.

Difference: the way in which places, populations and objects are not identical. It can be measured statistically, qualitatively and through the expression of opinions.

Feedback: the way that environmental changes become accelerated, or are negated, by the processes operating in a human or physical system.

Globalisation: the impact of world development on nations, regions, settlements and localities. The process by which the world is becoming increasingly interconnected as a result of increased integration and interdependence of the global economy.

Identity: how people view changing places from different perspectives and experiences. What a place means to them.

Inequality: social and economic (income and wealth) inequalities between people and places that Robert Schiller (Nobel Prize for Economics 2013) recognised as the greatest threat to society today.

Interdependence: relations of mutual dependence that are worldwide — the world economy, structure of trade, communications and production are interdependent.

Meaning: what a geographer understands from what is observed or imagined and the way that information is represented to the individual.

Mitigation: the reduction of a phenomenon that is having a negative effect on people, places or the environment.

Place: this is the most important concept to understand. It is a portion of geographic space occupied by a person or thing to which meaning has been given. It may have uniqueness and distinctiveness as a result of the way it has developed and changed. It is a place to which meaning has been ascribed. It is shaped by the relationships to other places and spaces at a range of scales. It is real and part of one's everyday life. Place has an identity, a personality and a position in space. Place has a layered history, a bit like geological strata, which builds up over time. Place can be defined by:

(a) its architecture — Georgian Bath and Clifton, Bristol

(b) its age — the nineteenth-century terraces of Abercanaid and Llwyn yr
    in Eos, Merthyr and Aberdare respectively

(c) the current or former economic base of the place —Shoreditch (silicon
    roundabout) and Ebbw Vale (iron and steel).

Representation: how a place or area is portrayed by formal agencies (the local council or tourist board) and people representing what they see and experience. How people are represented in a political sense. It may also refer to how a place is represented in literature and the media.

Resilience: the ability of an object or a population to adapt to changes that have a negative impact upon them.

Risk: the possibility of a range of possible outcomes resulting from a decision or a course of action that might affect people or the place. It exists when probabilities of outcomes are known from previous experience. It is a systematic way of dealing with society's modernisation and manufactured risks, such as pollution. It can also be natural risk in relation to natural hazards. These risks can combine, as in the case of Fukushima (earthquake, tsunami and radioactive pollution).

Scale: is familiar when it comes to maps, but it can also refer to coverage of an issue that may be in detail in one area but lacking detail in others. Scale can be used to compare similar sized areas, can be contextualised moving from the large to small scale and aggregated as one moves from small to larger areas.

Space: the area occupied by an object or objects, the distance between objects — basic in geography because of spatial distributions and spatial relationships.

Sustainability: development that meets the needs of the present without compromising the ability of future generations to meet their own needs. It is underpinned by two key concepts:

1 The needs for water, food and shelter are essential for the world's poor.
2 The state imposes limitations of technology and social organisation on the environment's ability to meet both present and future needs.

Systems: a set of interrelated objects. They can be either closed — no import or export of materials or energy — or open, where imports occur and are essential for the system.

Threshold: the minimum demand or population needed to support the provision of a good or service. A critical limit or level that must not be crossed in order to prevent a system from undergoing accelerated and potentially irreversible change. The tipping point for change within places.

Time: is a key element of change that can be noted at any scale whether it be short or long, from seconds to decades, centuries and geological time. Time can be related to distance between objects and people.

Fieldwork and the Non-Examination Assessment (NEA)

Whether you are studying for AS or A-level, you must spend a day on a fieldwork exercise related to Changing places. For A-level, your school/college will have to declare what you studied on a form, which will accompany your individual project (NEA). AS students will be asked a third question in the examination, which will cover the generic aspects of the work that you did in the field.

Fieldwork may lead to ideas for your individual investigation (NEA). The investigation can also arise from your other studies, whether it is an aspect of places or any of the rest of the core and option content. Some brief ideas for field study will be presented in each section of this guide.

Content Guidance

■ Changing places: relationships and connections

Getting started

On your journey to college or school, what types of urban or rural area do you pass through? One student may depart on a bus from a small development of 1980s houses, a small community, which the local residents' committee call a **village**, despite it being in an **exurb** of 17,000 people swallowed up by suburbia. Her journey takes her through an area of semi-detached homes built between 1920 and 1939, the residents of which voted solidly Conservative in the 2015 general election, and past a retail park. The bus enters a traditional **suburban** high street with small retailers, estate agents, charity shops, betting shops and a bingo hall in the former cinema. This 'high street' locality also houses some local and government offices. Her route continues past motor row — car sales showrooms on former military land, some of which is the location for new high-tech industries. Next, through nineteenth-century terraced housing with its corner shops, pubs turned into supermarket chain stores and a cinema converted into a mosque. Some of her friends from the South Asian communities board the bus. They are worried by the number of people in this **neighbourhood** who voted for the UK Independence Party (UKIP).

The bus takes the inner ring around the city centre, with its landscape of car parks surrounding the pedestrianised shopping area. She finally reaches her school, on the fringe of the old medieval town centre, abandoned as the central area over 100 years ago. This is the desirable part of the city (*neighbourhood*) to live in (*identity*) and it is close to the local university.

Exam tip

It is essential that you make copious use of your home place and the region in which it is located.

What characterises the places she identified? She identifies architecture (**landmarks**), the areas' cultural, social and demographic mix, and their economic profile. She is also recalling her own mental map based on the **pathway** that her journey takes. She has identified **edges** between **areas** where there is a defined change, such as around the city centre. She noted that places are dynamic because they adapt and change over time.

People use different terms for the places we live in. Some of these key definitions are:

- **Built-up area:** defined by the 2011 census as areas of built-up land that are joined together and where the gap between the developed land is less than 200 m. For example, Cardiff's built-up area includes Penarth, Pontypridd and Caerphilly.

- **City**: large settlement depending primarily on service and knowledge industries together with manufacturing. It is an aggregation of places. In 2015, UK cities made up 9% of the land area of the UK yet housed 54% of the population. 59% of jobs and 72% of the highly skilled workers live in them. 78% of new migrants live in cities. Officially, cities in the UK have been granted city status by royal charter. There are currently 69, of which 51 are in England and 6 in Wales. Some still cling to the idea that a city has to have a cathedral. However, these are historical definitions rather than definitions based on current functions, and hardly apply to many other countries.
- **City region**: area served by and functionally bound to a city and normally includes the journey to work and journey to study regions.
- **Community**: set of interacting but diverse groups of people found at a particular locality. It may be tied together by common heritage although many can be very diverse.
- **Conurbation**: urban area that has fused together over time, such as Greater Manchester or the Ruhr region of Germany. It may grow from one centre, e.g. London, or from several, e.g. the West Midlands.
- **Dispersed city**: US term used to define cities that have sprawled over a wide area, such as the spread of the San Francisco urban area around San Francisco Bay and up to 60 miles beyond into California.
- **Dormitory village** and **commuter village**: used to describe a settlement in which the population is socially urban and works in nearby urban areas. Estate agents frequently misappropriate the term to describe new developments and boost the attractiveness of neighbourhoods within cities.
- **Exurbia**: those areas beyond the urban area that house people who live in mainly rural surroundings but work in urban areas.
- **Global hubs**: large cities that are at the heart of the global economic and financial system, e.g. London, Tokyo, Shanghai, New York.
- **Hamlet**: small cluster of dwellings/farms lacking services.
- **Isolated dwellings**: single or pairs of rural dwellings, often in sparsely populated areas.
- **Locality**: descriptive term for where people live out their daily working and domestic lives. It can vary in size and geographers use the term loosely for anything from the small scale to a large urban area.
- **Megacity**: cities with very large populations, e.g. Shanghai, Tokyo, Mexico City.
- **Megalopolis**: growing together of large urban and suburban areas, e.g. Boswash, the area between Boston and Washington DC, USA.
- **Metropolitan area**: frequently used instead of conurbation.
- **Minor built-up rural area**: rural area with a main settlement of under 10,000 people.
- **Neighbourhood**: distinct and recognisable residential area that may be the location of home and its immediate environment. It can be someone else's home base and area. It is an area of similar housing, persons and lifestyles. It was used most obviously in the planning of new towns in the 1960s, having originated in the Garden City movement.
- **Primary Urban Area (PUA)**: built-up area of a city that invariably extends beyond its administrative area, used in publications of www.centreforcities.org.

Exam tip

You need to know and use the various place/settlement terms and definitions that are used by geographers.

- **Rural settlement**: village, hamlet and/or isolated farms in the countryside formerly associated with primary employment. Most of the population of rural settlements do not work in the countryside. Rural UK is psychologically urban because the hamlets and villages contain people who may have retired from a city job, or who work in nearby urban areas. Peter Hall stated in 2014 that there are few truly rural settlements within 150 miles of London.
- **Rural–urban fringe**: dated term that refers to the immediate surroundings of an urban area, which contains elements of an urban area, such as golf courses alongside open countryside.
- **Suburb**: area of mainly residential units that has been developed around the core of a town or city. It has increasingly contained other uses, such as industry, retailing, offices, recreational buildings and public open spaces.
- **Town**: small urban area with a range of services to serve an area that may include some independent retailers, schools (sometimes secondary), post offices, banks and estate agents.
- **Village**: small rural settlement with some functions, e.g. post office, shops, public houses and a church. Population sizes vary (200–7,000 in the UK but far larger in Italy, for example).
- **World city**: broader term than global hub that refers to cities which are prominent in the operation of the world economy, e.g. Hong Kong, Singapore, Frankfurt, Paris.

All of these terms are not entirely discrete because communities and localities are embedded in suburbs of cities or in villages. They nest within larger places and give those places a *meaning* because of the combination of localities or communities.

What makes a place distinct?

Arundel in West Sussex is a small former market town or large village. Living in the Arundel of 1960 was different yet similar in many ways to living in the Arundel of 2016 (*time*). The shops catered for local people and were locally owned. Greengrocers, butchers, bakers, a dairy, 'ladies and gents outfitters', two banks, a jewellers, a cinema and some small factories catered for the needs of the population. The Arundel Castle Estate, its farms and horse racing stables, provided employment for many, although some did commute by bus and train to London and nearby towns. There were many public houses and a former coaching inn. A council estate had just been completed on the fringe of the town (*identity*). Population had declined in the previous decade and 21% of the inhabitants were retired.

Arundel (population 3,285 in 2011) now functions as a tourist centre within the South Downs National Park. A more commercialised castle, a cathedral, jailhouse, museums and the Wild Fowl and Wetlands Trust are among its attractions. Its *identity* and *representation* changed through modernisation. The centre has many antique shops and small galleries, an antique bookshop and specialist food shops, together with a range of bars, the same coaching inn, and restaurants and cafés catering to all tastes, especially those of visitors.

However, its two banks are closing. The *threshold* population required to sustain their services grew to the point that local retailing and banking are no longer viable. A farmers' market has returned to the town, which is a Fair Trade town. Much of the population now commutes to work in larger towns by car and some

> ### Self-study task
>
> How would you categorise your home place? What size is it? What makes it distinct now and in the past? Does it have identity, personality and a unique location?

by rail to London. The retired population of the town has remained at 21%. The Office for National Statistics classifies Arundel as a 'coastal and countryside senior community' because its demography resembles nearby coastal places such as Littlehampton and Bognor Regis, and countryside places such as Petworth and Midhurst. Although it has changed as the economy has altered to a service economy due to the growth of tourism, the identity of the main street and most of the streets in the old town has not changed. However, while the buildings are identical, their functions have changed. Therefore, the differences in 2016 are not architectural but social and economic. Nevertheless, the architecture enables the town to continue to function as a tourist centre; it is **resilient**.

Clovelly, Cornwall has changed its economic base yet its visual image remains the same. Once primarily a mackerel fishing small harbour at the mouth of a steep valley, with houses clinging to the valley sides and cliff edge, the village has become a tourist hot spot that is still *represented* by the village's personality as a harbour. Mackerel fishing, now strictly controlled by EU fishing policy, has declined to just one boat, but tourism has boomed. External forces have changed Clovelly's economic base, but the image of the place remains resilient.

Place can be a larger area that can be seen in different ways.

Continuity and change in the Lake District

James Rebanks recalled listening in 1987 to a school assembly when a teacher talked about the Lake District where he was the son of a sheep farmer.

> 'I realised that curiously she knew, and claimed to love, our land. But she talked about it … in terms that were completely alien to my family and me. She loved a "wild" landscape, full of mountains, lakes, leisure and adventure, lightly peopled with folk I had never met. The Lake District in her monologue was the playground for an itinerant band of climbers, poets, walkers and daydreamers … people whom, unlike our parents, or us, had 'really done something'. Occasionally she would utter a name in a reverential tone and look in vain for us to respond with interest. One was Alfred Wainwright, another Chris Bonnington; and she kept going on about someone called Wordsworth. … Sitting in that assembly was the first time I'd encountered this romantic way of looking at our landscape. I realised that the landscape we loved, where we had belonged for centuries, the place known as The Lake District, had a claim to ownership submitted by other people, based on principles I barely understood.
>
> But, above all I would learn that our landscape changed the rest of the world. It is where the idea that all of us have a direct sense of 'ownership' (regardless of property rights) of some places or things because they are beautiful, or stimulating, or just special was put into words. …
>
> Above all, … I learnt that we are not the only ones that love this place. It is, for better or worse, a scenic playground for the rest of Britain, and for countless other people from around the world. I simply had to travel over the fell to Ullswater to see the cars streaming past on the roads or the crowds milling around the shore of the lake, to see what this means. …

Self-study task

How does Arundel differ from your home place? Are there any changes that are similar or completely different? List the similarities and differences using headings such as: size, population characteristics, age of buildings, functions. Think about how and why your place is changing.

Today 16 million people a year come here to an area with 43,000 residents. Many farms depend upon tourism for the income and running. In some valleys 60–70% of the houses are second homes or holiday cottages, so that many local people cannot afford to live in their own communities. The locals speak begrudgingly of being "outnumbered" and all of us know that we are in every way a tiny minority in this landscape. The teacher's idea of the Lake District was created by an urbanised and increasingly industrialised society over the past 200 years. It was a dream of a place for a wider society that was full of people disconnected from the land. That dream was never for us, the people who work this land. We were already here doing what we do.'

Copyright James Rebanks (2015),
reproduced by permission of Penguin Books Ltd.

Try to describe in your own words the two versions of the Lake District as a place in this excerpt.

Continuity and change in contrasting places

'Cannery Row in Monterey in California is a poem, a stink, a grating noise, a quality of light, a tone, a habit, a nostalgia, a dream.'

John Steinbeck, *Cannery Row*, Penguin Modern Classics (1945)

This description of Cannery Row, written in 1945 but describing the place in the 1930s, is different to the place we see 80 years later. Go to www.canneryrow.com to see how it has changed. Steinbeck's representation is used to give *meaning* and *identity* to a tourist centre today.

Perhaps there are other rural and urban communities where the place is given contrasting meanings. For instance, there are different meanings applied to both the daytime and night time (when the nightclub economy is in full swing) in Market Street, Cardiff and the Bigg Market, Newcastle.

Fieldwork

It is possible to gather data and descriptions of a place (through interviewing, qualitative skills and recording of oral history) from its elderly residents in order to examine what factors have caused a place to change and how this has affected the people living there.

Foster City, California

A **contrasting place** is Foster City, California (Figure 1). Foster City is an affluent, planned settlement of 32,377 people (2013) built on reclaimed marshland on the western shore of San Francisco Bay. Jack Foster bought Brewer Island and the surrounding wetlands in 1958, drained it and raised its level by dredging $10.7\,m^3$ of sands and muds from the Bay.

Knowledge check 1

Can you identify or suggest technological, economic, demographic and political factors that have brought about the changes noted by Rebanks?

Exam tip

You need to have knowledge of at least one contrasting place. You could contrast the example above with your home place.

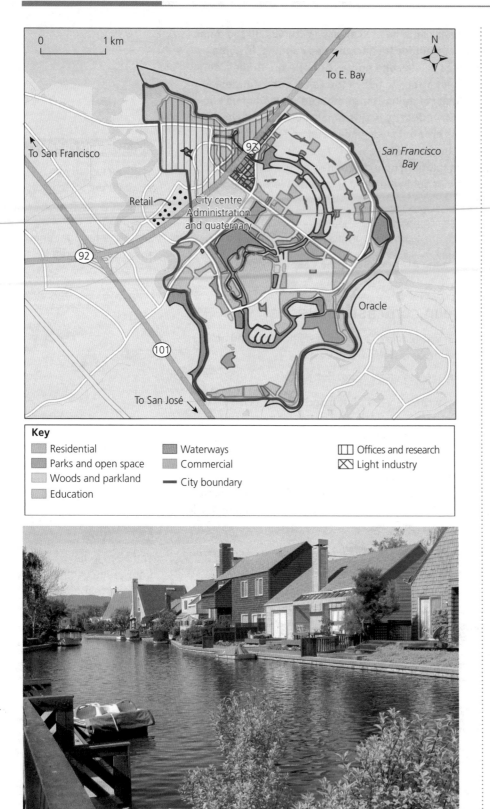

Key

▨ Residential	▨ Waterways	▥ Offices and research
▨ Parks and open space	▨ Commercial	⊠ Light industry
▨ Woods and parkland	— City boundary	
▨ Education		

Figure 1 Foster City, California

Today the place is distinct because it is an urban area defined and given identity by the Bay and Belmont Slough, a tidal watercourse. The site has 86ha, or 16 miles, of sea water lagoons and the Slough, created when the city was first developed. The local people navigate these with small (electric, sail or human-powered) vessels.

The 'city' covers 97,346ha. It is primarily a medium- to high-earner residential community (Figure 1) although, with the passage of time, the proportion of the retired population is growing. There is no city centre in a European sense; it only houses the city administration and regional offices for Visa and IBM. There are several small retail areas but the main shopping is in malls either at the edge of or beyond the city limits. Employment is often elsewhere, leading to a daily outflow of commuters to Silicon Valley headquarters (see page 60). Quaternary work and the knowledge economy dominate, as firms move into the area and cluster near the main road access routes from the dispersed Bay City. By 2015, 16,000 people worked here, many commuting in from cities in the Bay area.

The population composition enhances the uniqueness (*identity*) of Foster City. In 2013, 46% were of Asian origin, the majority of whom were born in China (including Hong Kong), India, Japan and Taiwan (*interdependence*). They have the highest average earnings. The white US and European population is 41% of the total (20% were born outside of the USA and only 38% born in California). A further 6.5% are Hispanic, a far lower proportion than in the rest of California. The African-American population is 2.1% of the total; on average, they are the lowest earners. Foster City is a city of immigrants with a multicultural identity. The cost of living here is 2.5 times that of the US average. The average income is US$160,000 and house prices average US$1m (approximately £750,000, 2016) and rise to US$2.5m (approximately £1.90m).

An **object** can sometimes define the identity of a place. The 'Google bicycle' (Figure 2) is used by 13,000 employees at the Mountain View California HQ to cycle between its buildings. The buildings' functions are not posted outside and therefore the parked bicycles (*representation*) give a spatial extent to the 'Google Campus'. A Google journey to work region can also be defined by the extent of the routes that the frequent free Google buses, which bring employees to work from up to 60 miles away, follow.

The Brixton pound (£) is a locally accepted banknote, and is used to try and retain spending in Brixton, south London rather than beyond the place. The place in which the note, with its image of a local popular icon, David Bowie, can be spent defines the spatial extent of Brixton (*representation*).

Figure 2 The Google bicycle

Knowledge check 2

Do you have examples of other places that are defined by objects? Are there other places in the UK that can be defined by their own currency?

Factors that shape the changing identity and characteristics of places

Table 1 lists the factors that affect the changing identity of places ranging from villages and neighbourhoods to regions.

Table 1 Factors that affect the changing identity of places

Factors	Village	Neighbourhood	Suburbs	City centre	Region
Cultural	New economy	Community-based	Segregation	Leisure quarter	—
Economic	Decline of primary and rise of service employment	Adaptation to new or existing demographic	Industrial estates/office parks	Tertiary and quaternary growth; R&D	Deindustrialisation; Global changes e.g. the web, multinational companies
Investment	Global investors; New rural economy	Renovation	Renovation	New retail and leisure	Inward investment/FDI, infrastructure investment
Resources	New land uses	Community-based: specialist retail	—	Knowledge industries: universities	Accessibility nationally and internationally
Demographic	Ageing population	Homogeneity	Ageing, diverse communities	Reurbanisation, gentrification	Unemployment, deprivation
Migration	Young leave and mature move in	Nest builders	Life cycle moves, social segregation	Student flats	In- and out-migration

Factors	Village	Neighbourhood	Suburbs	City centre	Region
Planning	Expanded settlement: counter-urbanisation	Garden City, neighbourhood units	Green belts	Redevelopment	Development grants
Political	NIMBYism	Neighbourhood Watch	—	Rebranding boosterism	Government Regional Policies
Global forces	Global agricultural production	Satellite TV	Retail e.g. ASDA and McDonald's	Global banks, financial companies, leisure chains; Private involvement	FDI

How does continuity and change affect lives?

Bermondsey, south of the River Thames and situated between London Bridge and Tower Bridge, has experienced many changes that affect lives. The poor inhabited the area even in Shakespeare's time, when the area straddled the road south from the only Thames crossing. It had markets, e.g. Borough Market; wharves along the Thames, which were London's sole docks; and noxious industries, such as tanning, taverns, brothels, coaching inns and slums, which inspired Charles Dickens' *Oliver Twist*.

By the nineteenth century rail routes crossed the area (which, in the twentieth century, now enclose areas of municipal housing that replaced some of the slums). Industry grew, including a gas works, printing and food processing of goods imported through the port.

In the Second World War, much of the area was destroyed during the Blitz. These areas then became a focus for council housing as a result of comprehensive renewal (*causality*). The docks grew derelict because of new shipping technologies further downstream.

In the 1980s, the London Docklands Development Corporation (LDDC) began to redevelop the area. Commercial developments were housed in converted buildings and private investment attracted a middle-class population into converted warehouses. On the western fringes, the Globe Theatre (1996) and Tate Modern (2000) became part of the South Bank cultural complex. Jobs in the traditional industries declined, replaced by public services and creative industries. By 2011, the population was more cosmopolitan and socially polarised in one of the most deprived areas of the capital (*adaptation* and *time*).

Serena, an unemployed mother living on a Bermondsey a council estate (*community*), states: 'Everybody on the estate knows everybody else. The estate is hospitable because it is small [*attachment*]. Other estates don't have community because they are tall blocks. People tend not to give up their flats on this estate.'

In contrast, Henrietta, a management software consultant, lives in a warehouse conversion at Butler's Wharf: 'I love it here — going for a coffee, to the bakery and a drink at All Bar One and to the good restaurants [*identity*]. The flats are really expensive but you would not talk to the people in the lift.'

These two experiences illustrate how change in the area has affected people's lives in different ways.[1]

1 The quotes are adapted from Hall, Peter (2007) *London Voices, London Lives*, The Policy Press. The text contains many interviews about changing places across London.

Fieldwork

Interview residents in a neighbourhood near where you live to see how changes in the economy and society have influenced their lives. Find out whether they feel safe, whether they have noticed that the neighbours have changed from when they first lived there and what work people undertake today. Try to establish why they feel the way they do. A good case study is the move of West Ham FC to the Olympic Park and its impact on the area around the former Boleyn Ground, which depended on trade from football fans and is due to be redeveloped.

Self-study task

If you have lived in the same area all of your life, what aspects of the area have changed and what have remained constant? How and why have these changes affected you? Is it because you are older or your interests have changed?

Events and decisions at a global level can affect people at a local level

In the past, decisions made at a national scale affected people, whereas today, global-level decisions affect local people. Worldwide **interdependence** occurs due to the nature of the modern global economy, trade patterns and communications.

In 2015, Volkswagen (VW) was found to have breached regulations concerning emissions from cars. This resulted in fewer people purchasing VW vehicles. The main VW car plant, in Wolfsburg, Germany, employs 70,000 workers, all of whom received a profit bonus of €5,900 (£4,900) in 2014. The bonus did not occur in 2015 as the firm was forced to cover the costs of selling fewer cars. Business in the city that depended on VW employees' spending also had to readjust; for example, osteopaths and chiropractors forecast a 25% drop in patient numbers and income. Redundancy hit shops, supply firms and other services. Workers took fewer holidays, which had an impact on the local tourism economy. The communities in an around Wolfsburg were also affected.

Many global companies are involved in a wide variety of activities and retailing in cities. Table 2 shows the ownership of some well-known shops.

Table 2 Non-UK ownership of selected functions in UK cities

Name	Type of activity and retailers owned	Where owned
Aldi	Discount supermarket	Family in Germany
Lidl	Discount supermarket	Germany
Asda Stores	Supermarket	Walmart Group Arkansas, USA
McDonald's	Fast food	Oak Brook, Illinois, USA
Starbucks	Coffee shop	Seattle, USA
House of Fraser	Department store	Nanjing, China
Waterstones	Bookseller	Russian owner
Accor	Hotels: Mercure, Novotel, Ibis, Mama Shelter, Sofitel and F1	Paris, France
Domino's Pizza	Fast food	Ann Arbor, Michigan, USA
Arcadia Group	Debenhams, Topshop, Topman, Burton, Dorothy Perkins, Evans, Miss Selfridge, Wallis and the out-of-town chain Outfit	London, UK
Hony Capital	Pizza Express, Zizi, ASK Italian	Beijing, China

Knowledge check 3

What does Table 2 suggest about the interdependence of cities with the global economy?

Summary

- Place is a part of everyone's life and we all give different places different meanings.
- Its identity will be seen differently by different age groups, genders and those who seek to manage and represent the place on our behalf.
- Places adapt and change over time and contain elements whose identity has been modified by new social and economic events.
- People become attached to places at a variety of scales.
- Places are interdependent increasingly as a consequence of globalisation.
- Always be able to use your home places to illustrate points.

Changing places: meaning and representation

How are places given meaning and represented by people?

People view places differently as a consequence of their age, economic status, ethnicity, gender, ideology, language, politics, race, religion and social class. Jerusalem is a different place whether you are a Jew, Muslim or Christian. It is a divided city whose divisions reflect the engagement of the Palestinian and Jewish populations with the city over time (*difference*).

Self-study task

How are gated communities (residential complexes/areas where access is through controlled access points and electronic gates) viewed by those who live there and those living beyond them? How might students and the elderly view Ibiza? Such changing or contrasting perceptions may have economic, cultural and political consequences.

- In Gateshead, teenagers expressed a fear of certain areas in the town and girls (*gender*) were more fearful, despite evidence that they were less victimised.
- Visitors to a place perceive it differently from residents (*economic status, social class, language*).
- In another study, Asian and Afro-Caribbean 16–24-year-olds felt safe in the terraced housing community where they lived (*race, ethnicity,* and *age*) whereas other ethnic groups felt unsafe there, especially at night.

Fieldwork

What makes a place safe? Contrast the perceptions of different age groups of an area, or areas, of your home town/village. Do tourists' perceptions of a place differ to those of the local population?

The meaning and representation of Chichester Harbour Area of Outstanding Natural Beauty

Chichester Harbour, an Area of Outstanding Natural Beauty (AONB), encompasses a wide range of environments and urban places within its 74 square kilometres. It was established in law in 1971, and administers the area and produces plans for its future. The AONB (Figure 3) contains coastal villages, e.g. Bosham and West Wittering, and is fringed by former market towns such as Emsworth, Havant (a suburb of Portsmouth) and the seaside resort of Hayling Island. People's perceptions of this place vary considerably, and how they identify with it will depend on how they perceive where they live and the experiences they undergo in that *locality*. There are several groups who attribute *meaning* to the AONB:

- The Chichester Harbour Conservancy: produces the management plan and administers the AONB. It belongs, politically, to two county areas, West Sussex and Hampshire (*politics, ideology*)

   'The importance of conserving the natural environment remains central to our work.'

   Chichester Harbour Conservancy (2015) *News & Guide.*

- **Residents**: there are 10,502 residents of the communities within the AONB; their numbers grew by 25% between 1991 and 2014. Average income is £38,570 and 30% are over the age of 60. A portion of their council tax goes towards maintaining the harbour (*economic status, social class, age, gender*).
- **Second-home owners**: form 25% of the housing stock (*economic status, social class*).
- **Parish councils**: concerned about sea level rises, and sewage generated by the increasing number of homes (*politics*).

■ **Recreational visitors and tourists**: there are 1.5 million recreational and tourist visits per year. 45% of these visitors travel from under 10 miles away, mainly to sail (*economic status, social class*).

■ **Sailing clubs and educational activity centres**: boat owners pay harbour dues and mooring fees (*age, gender, economic status, social class*).

■ **Organisations managing environmental conservation**: includes the National Trust, Natural England and those who administer Local Nature Reserves and Sites of Special Scientific Interest (SSSIs). These organisations know that management is within the context of a 5.2 mm/year rise in mean sea level since 1991 (*ideology, politics*).

■ **15 farms** (*economic status, politics*).

■ **Friends of Chichester Harbour**: 3,000 members (*ideology, social class*).

■ **Chichester Harbour Trust**: an independent charity created to conserve this area of unspoilt estuary and its surrounding landscape for the public benefit.

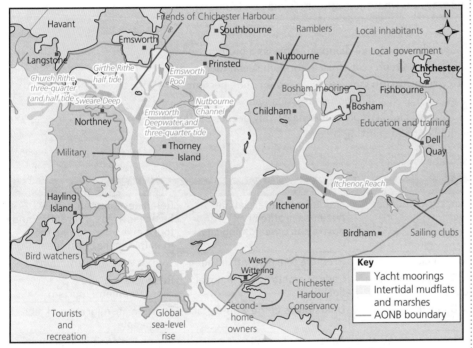

Figure 3 Chichester Harbour Area of Outstanding Natural Beauty and the pressures on the area

Table 3 Engagement with and perception of the Chichester Harbour AONB

Group/ organisation	Engagement with harbour	How harbour locality is perceived	Experiences that influence perception of place
Local residents			
Second-home owners			
Yacht clubs			
Parish Council			
Conservancy			
Farmers			

Knowledge check 4

For each of the groups listed in Table 3, copy and complete the columns to illustrate how people engage with the harbour as a place and perceive what is happening, and the experiences that may have influenced some members of that group to engage with and perceive the harbour area.

Representations of place in advertising and promotional material through different media and publications

How is your school or college represented in publications? Promotional material can be in the form of a hardcopy or digital prospectus, social media, local newspaper reports of examination success, expansion and events, and official reports on the quality of education and statistics in league tables. All of these sources represent a place.

At a larger scale, the same is true for the place in which you live. Find out how many different sources of information represent the place in which you live. You need to be aware of which groups author these representations of place, why they are presented this way and what their outcomes may be (Table 4).

Table 4 lists a selection of groups who use the media to advertise and promote the city of Portsmouth. Individuals can also represent a place, through social media such as Facebook and Instagram. **Representation** can also be based on one's personal experience on a single occasion, such as visual impressions when house hunting, a traffic jam and certain events. A place can be represented negatively because it floods, or positively because of individual or team sporting success.

Table 4 A selection of representations of Portsmouth

Source	Who	Why	Outcomes
City Council	The party in political power	Maintain commercial and business profile of city; portray as a welcoming city	Retail developments, new business areas, recreation and tourism income; taking more than fair share of refugees
Visit Portsmouth	City Council	Promote tourism with images	Tourist visits to attractions
investinportsmouth.co.uk	City Council, business groups	Loss of employment in naval dockyard	Regeneration and redevelopment; tourism
Waterfront & Island City	City Council	Uniqueness of the whole place	Tourism; in-migration of jobs and people
Portsmouth FC	Community-owned club	Advertise club following financial crises	Improving position lost after 2010; team's supporters as a community
University of Portsmouth	University, its governors, Universities UK	Status in UK and overseas	League table position; staff and student recruitment; the student spend
International ferry port	City/ferry and shipping companies	Employment and trade; three sites of commercial docks	Tourism including cruises; imports (bananas)
Cathedrals	Roman Catholic and Anglican churches	Community and spiritual involvement	Talks on ethics —community awareness
Muslim communities	Two mosques	Spiritual involvement; try to dispel media image regarding fundamentalism	Inter- and intra-community harmony
Portsmouth Sixth Form College	College and its governors	Role in city community; recruitment	Equal opportunity college; enhanced status in city; a learning community

Source	Who	Why	Outcomes
Clinical Commissioning Group	24 GP surgeries	Health of population	Healthy employable population; prestige
IBM	Major employer	Global company invested in area for 50 years	Do not say they are in Portsmouth but their location is in North Harbour; attract employees
BAE Systems	Defence industry in naval dockyard	Loss of shipbuilding	Government investment in naval ship repairing and servicing; maintains some jobs
The National Trust	National interest group	Potential for city to be at flood risk from global warming	Saving homes and jobs in an island city
Americas Cup Consortium	BAR and Land Rover; Ben Ainsley	Investment and publicity; good location for boat racing	Major world sporting event; jobs and income to region; prestige in UK and abroad

Self-study task

Draw up your own table showing how a place that you know is represented. Which representations appeal to you, your family and other age groups? Why do they differ?

Exam tip

Make sure that you have gained the ability to interpret photographic evidence of change in unfamiliar places. The photographs can be ground-level images, or oblique and/or vertical aerial photos, or satellite imagery.

Contrasting images portrayed by and between the formal statistical, media and popular images of places

Go to www3.hants.gov.uk/2011_census_portsmouth_summary_factsheet.pdf, which provides the formal statistical summary for Portsmouth. It contains detail on population, age groups, dependency ratios, marital status, country of birth, ethnicity, tenure, religion and household composition. Contrast the data with the image presented by local media, i.e. www.portsmouth.co.uk. Are they reporting the same place by emphasising crime, football matches, road crashes and local protests about closure of facilities? What photographs and maps are used?

Self-study task

Carry out a similar exercise for your own place. How do different groups, statistics and media represent it? What identity is given to the place and how is it represented to you? Is the place adapting or responding to risk, and does it contain resilient communities? Why are the images contrasting?

Personal images of places vary and affect the way people react to other unfamiliar places

You have built up your own personal image of a place, which will differ from other individuals' images. Your image might be a map, a photograph or a painting. How far would you agree with C. S. Lewis when he states in his book *The Chronicles of Narnia* that 'Girls … never carry maps in their head'?

Images of a place might alter with age, and with the way that you travel around a place whether by car or public transport. The *meaning* of places can alter with your value

Self-study task

Do members of your class have different maps or images of a place/s?

system — the dominance of a building such as the Principality Stadium, Cardiff or The Shard, London may be viewed negatively among those with a conservative value system whereas those with a more liberal set of values may react positively.

Fieldwork

Find out which are the priciest, or the cheapest, roads to live on, in a place near you. Table 5 lists a selection of the most expensive and cheapest streets on which to buy a home (taken from various newspaper articles in 2015). Using data from Rightmove or Zoopla for your own place, find out the characteristics that make a road's housing expensive or cheap. Try to visit these streets. A similar exercise could contrast the characteristics of other streets with a near-average value for the place.

Table 5 A selection of the most expensive and cheapest streets for housing outside of London

Place	Most expensive streets	Place	Cheapest streets
Cobham, Surrey	Icklingham Rd, Harebell Hill	Clacton-on-Sea	Austin Ave.
Sandbanks, Poole	Sandbanks Rd, Western Ave., Haig Ave.	Burnley	Elmwood St., Spencer St., Colville St., Norman St., Hurtley St
Cambridge	Newton Rd, CB2 and CB3	Ferryhill, Darlington	Haig St.
Prestbury, Macclesfield	Castle Hill	Bootle	Shakespeare St.
Wilmslow	Torkington Rd	Stockton-on-Tees	Limetree Close
Gosforth, Newcastle	Graham Park Rd	Mountain Ash	Fernhill
Harrogate	Rutland Drive	Ebbw Vale	Brynwelor
Stratford-upon-Avon	Tiddington Rd	Penarth	Cwrt-Y-Vil Rd
Cardiff	Druidstone Rd, Rudry Rd, Llyswen Rd, Lisvane Rd		
Swansea	Lady Housty Ave., Langland Court Rd		
Penarth	Cwrt-Y-Vil Rd		

In examining the characteristics of these streets, you should research the following factors:

- the age of property in the area
- the current and past economic status of the area
- the size and upkeep of the properties and the street
- whether your age, gender and where you live and have lived affect how you assess these characteristics.

Self-study task

Figures 4 and 5 show two distinct urban areas. Describe these areas in terms of their identity, demography, and age of buildings and architecture, and suggest the possible lifestyles that are associated with them. How will these areas be perceived and represented by those living in other parts of Poole (Figure 4) and Merseyside (Figure 5)?

Exam tip

Whenever possible, you should use examples that are developed from your familiarity with a place.

Figure 4 An area of Poole

Figure 5 An area of Merseyside

Summary

- People will represent places differently.
- Frequently, interest groups will give meaning to a place that backs up their own ideas and ideology.
- The media portray places and give them identity as a result of the events and stories that they select to publish.
- Local government and companies will also attempt to portray a place in the most favourable light in order to boost the image of the place or company.
- People may define a place in their minds based on their knowledge of similar places that they know.

Changes over time in the economic characteristics of places

Models of economic and employment change in places over time

The **Clark Fisher Model** is a stylised way of describing the changing balance of employment over time, and has been used mainly at a national level. The model (Figure 6) distinguishes four sectors of the economy:

1 **Primary**: the part of the economy concerned with the collection and use of natural resources

2 **Secondary**: the manufacturing or industrial sector — the part that processes resources into goods that people want

3 **Tertiary**: the sector that enables goods to be traded, sometimes called producer services — includes wholesaling, retailing, banking, finance and insurance, transport, and entertainment, including tourism and personal services

4 **Quaternary**: research and development, and the knowledge economy, including IT, education and the processing of information

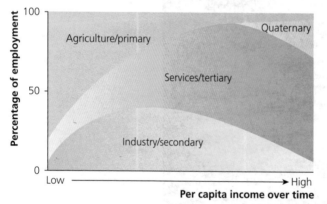

Figure 6 The modified Clark Fisher Model

In 2015, the Office for National Statistics (ONS) only distinguished the following:

- Agriculture and Fishing (Primary)
- Manufacturing (Secondary)
- Services (Tertiary and Quaternary)
- Construction (Secondary)

Note: the bracketed terms are those used in the Clark Fisher Model.

Self-study task

Summarise what you know about employment in your home place in this decade. You should be able to obtain details from the 2011 census and from local publications promoting your place/area. Using former censuses, historic maps and reports, describe how it has changed over time. For many places it will be useful to go back to the nineteenth century and identify significant changes in the economic character of your home place.

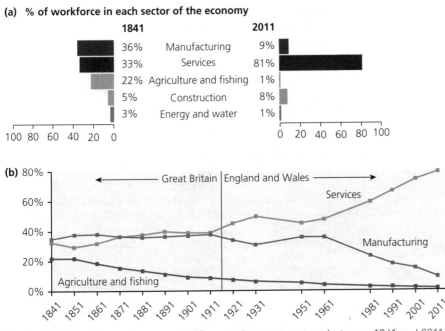

(a) % of workforce in each sector of the economy

1841		2011
36%	Manufacturing	9%
33%	Services	81%
22%	Agriculture and fishing	1%
5%	Construction	8%
3%	Energy and water	1%

Figure 7 (a) The changes between the five employment sectors between 1841 and 2011, and (b) the percentage of the workforce by employment sector between 1841 and 2011

Figure 7 shows how the balance of employment has changed over the past 160 years. **Kondratiev waves** (Figure 8 and Table 6) are another model used to describe the economic changes over time at a national level. Kondratiev waves are approximately 50 years in duration and each of the four past waves (K1–K4) has four phases: prosperity, recession, depression and recovery. Each wave is associated with the development of particular technological innovations and economic activities. The model ignores primary production. Some of these waves will have affected your home region and places within it.

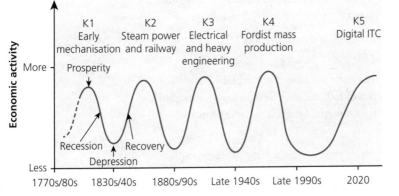

Figure 8 Kondratiev waves

These two models help to explain the changing dominance of activities in urban areas and, to a lesser extent, rural communities. Industrialisation is the process through which a society develops an economy based on mass and the mechanical production of goods. During the Industrial Revolution, an explosion of population and growth in

Exam tip

Demonstrate your knowledge of these waves when discussing the changing economy and society of places through time.

urban areas located close to each other and around transport nodes, such as ports and coalfields, led to rapid urbanisation. But the advent of electricity in the third Kondratiev wave enabled manufacturing to spread beyond cities and onto cheaper land.

Table 6 The five Kondratiev waves

Waves	1st	2nd	3rd	4th	5th
Main industries and/or economic activities	Water power; textiles; iron; potteries	Steam engines/ships; iron and steel; coalmining	Electrical engineering; heavy engineering; armaments; steel ships; chemicals; dyes	Automobiles; lorries; consumer durables; synthetic materials; petrochemicals	Computers; digital technology; internet; software; optical fibres; robotics; biotechnology; universities; R&D; creative industries
Transport and communication innovations	Canals; turnpikes	Railways; steamships	Electricity supply	Highways; airports	Digital; satellites; fibre optics; wi-fi; the Cloud
UK place examples	Manchester; Bradford; Stoke	Consett; Ebbw Vale; Aberdare; Glasgow	Birmingham; Birkenhead; Port Sunlight	Dagenham; Luton; Billingham	Silicon Roundabout (Old Street); Shoreditch; Cambridge; Menai Hub
Other world places	Lille; Verviers	Ruhr cities	Ludwigshafen	Detroit; Wolfsburg; Eindhoven	Silicon Valley; Bangalore

Cardiff

Cardiff grew between 1801 and 1901 from a city of 1,870 people living within the confines of the medieval walled town to an industrial city of 164,333. The growth of steam coal mining and iron production (second Kondratiev wave) gave rise to Cardiff becoming a major coal exporting port. The role of the wealthy Bute family in digging the canal and building the docks, and the coming of the railways between 1836 and 1853, aided the growth of the port and the city. The working population grew rapidly due to immigration. In 1851, approximately one-third of Cardiff's inhabitants came from Glamorgan and Monmouth, the surrounding counties. Others came from West Wales, Gloucestershire and Somerset. Most notable were the Irish fleeing famine in Ireland, who ended up living in overcrowded conditions in Splotlands and Newtown, described in 1855 as follows:

> 'It has a low level; the houses for the most part are occupied as Irish lodging-houses and are seriously overcrowded.'

The residential areas that were developed at this time became more socially segregated. Bute Town had a high concentration of lodgers and Grangetown contained poor housing, whereas Canton, Cathays and Roath were fast-growing areas housing those who were more affluent.

What factors can be identified leading to the changing economic base of nineteenth-century Cardiff?

- Population increase was rapid due to better disease control.
- Migration due to people being pushed by famine and rural poverty towards jobs and earnings, digging the docks, building homes and working in the new trading and commercial world of the city.

■ The role of individuals such as the Bute family, which used its wealth to invest and increase its own wealth. In other places, philanthropic employers set up model settlements, e.g. Titus Salt's Saltaire, Lever's Port Sunlight, Cadbury's Bourneville and Rowntree's New Earswick. Were they utopian or were they a means to control the workforce?

■ Transport developments enabled exports and trade to rise and made it easier to reach the city and its docks.

Other cities in the UK grew more rapidly than Cardiff. The textile industry in Lancashire sucked in labour and housed workers in terraced housing and back courts. Oldham grew from 21,000 in 1801 to 137,000 in 1901, and Manchester from 75,000 to 544,000 in the same period. Figure 5 (page 27) shows the type of housing typical of that period.

Knowledge check 5

Do you know the meaning 'of utopian'?

Fieldwork

Examine the modern social and architectural character of an area of nineteenth-century housing in your home town. How and why has it changed? It might be a student district today or an area that is home to a BME (black and minority ethnic) group.

This exercise involves both secondary data from past maps and surveys, and acquiring social data for the present character from the census, and processing it.

Location quotient

Location quotient (LQ) is a statistic that measures a region's industrial specialisation and concentration relative to a larger geographic unit (normally a country). An LQ is calculated as the share of an industry of the regional total for an economic statistic (number of factories, employment, etc.) divided by the industry's share of the national total for the same statistic. For example, an LQ of 1.0 means that the region and the nation are equally specialised in an activity, whereas an LQ of 1.8 means that the region has a higher concentration than the nation and an LQ of 0.5 means that it has a lower concentration. LQ is calculated using the following formula:

$$LQ = \frac{\text{\% of the total workforce in the area working in an activity}}{\text{the workforce in that activity in the country as a percentage of the total workforce}}$$

Industrialisation led to concentrations of manufacturing, such as that of textiles, in the nineteenth century. The following LQs were calculated for employment in the textile industries in 1861 in England:

Table 7 Location quotients (LQs) for textile industries in England and Wales, 1861

Industry	Gender	England: most clustered	England: second most clustered
Woollens	M	W. Riding, Yorks 7.9	Wiltshire 2.2
Woollens	F	W. Riding, Yorks 6.7	Wiltshire 4.7
Worsted	M	W. Riding, Yorks 8.8	Leicestershire 2.6
Worsted	F	W. Riding, Yorks 9.2	—
Cotton	M	Lancashire 4.9	Cheshire 2.1
Cotton	F	Lancashire 3.9	Cheshire 2.0

The data indicates that the woollen and worsted industry was much more clustered in the West Riding of Yorkshire compared with other counties.

Self-study task

LQ calculation

Complete the data for the South East and Wales in Table 1 on page 114. Which region has the nearest concentration of skilled tradespeople to the national average? Can you offer an explanation for the variations in concentration?

External forces and factors influencing economic restructuring

Ebbw Vale is a place that has been affected by the forces of economic change over the past 200 years (*time*). Ebbw grew as a product of the Industrial Revolution when an ironworks, powered by the coal extracted from the mines in the valley, was established in the region in the 1790s. In the 1860s, it became a centre for steel-making and a classic case of a plant based on coal energy supplies, using locally quarried limestone in the blast furnaces and becoming increasingly reliant on imported iron ore.

In the Depression years of the 1930s there was a decline in demand for coal and only 1% of the work remained in service. The Special Area Act 1934 attempted to rectify economic inactivity, unemployment, poor communications, poor housing and low skill levels in the region. However, an entrepreneur, aided by government grants, built the first integrated steel mill in Europe at Ebbw Vale, which used a new American technology known as continuous hot-rolling (*changing technology*). In 1947, tin plating was added to the works and upgraded in 1978 (*mitigation*). At its peak, the site supported a workforce of 16,000. However, by the 1970s the steel works generated high costs because it had to import ores from overseas and transfer them by rail to the site. It became cheaper to import steel from overseas, and as a result, Ebbw Vale was unable to find a market (*globalisation*). All steel production ceased in 1977–78 and the steelworks was demolished in 1981. Tin plating continued until 2001–02, when it was finally shut down. The resultant site/place was described as 'a 2-mile scar in the heart of a town'.

Long before the whole site was closed, Ebbw Vale bid to be a National Garden Festival site in 1992. The former iron and steel works site housed the Festival for six months. Since then, 'The Works' (Figure 9) has been redeveloped for housing, education (a 3–16-year-olds school and Coleg Gwent for post-16 education), retail (Festival Park) and a hospital (*government strategies*) with £350m investment aid from the EU. In 2010, the cooling ponds were converted to be a wetland centre (*environmental sustainability*). A museum has been opened in the old works offices. The Works is a 6.2ha site within the 38ha Enterprise Zone in the modern administrative area of Blaenau, Gwent. Enterprise Zone status (page 43) enables the designated areas to attract capital allowances from the government and funds for SMEs (small- and medium-enterprises) from Finance Wales. The Master Plan is an 'improvement from within' approach, i.e. if you provide space and improve education

Exam tip

You must be prepared to calculate data and apply formulae such as location quotients in an examination. If you cannot complete statistical or mathematical work in the time allowed, do not waste further time trying to answer the question, as it will likely count for no more than 5 marks at most.

and skills, business will locate here and the place will improve (*mitigation*). However, this ignores global economic development conditions, which have not been favourable since the 1990s. In 2015, Ebbw Vale and the Heads of the Valleys towns (e.g. Merthyr Tydfil and Tredegar) continued to be characterised by high concentrations of social deprivation and economic inactivity, poor health, low levels of attainment (40% unemployed or unavailable for work in 2016) and skills, and depopulation (*lifestyles, risk*).

Self-study task

In the EU Referendum, 62% voted 'leave', in spite of all this investment in infrastructure. Why have so many in a community that benefited from EU investment made that decision?

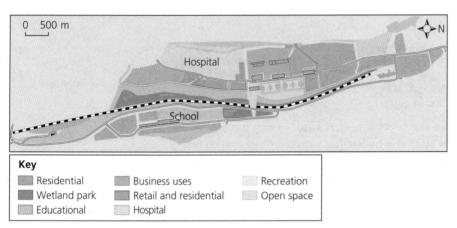

Figure 9 The Works, Ebbw Vale

What factors have brought about the economic changes outlined for this place (*mitigation*)?

- **Technological changes**: changes in iron and steel-making, tin-plating and transport technologies; introducing new technologies and pharmaceuticals
- **Government strategies**: at local (Blaenau, Gwent), regional/national (Wales/UK) and EU/international level (Special Areas Act 1934, Development Areas, Enterprise Zones, Garden Festivals, ERDF Structural Funds, creating new education facilities)
- **Resource depletion**: original iron sources, coal supplies costly; cheaper imports to coastal steel works (*sustainability*)
- **Economies of scale**: unable to compete with larger, often coastal plants, in both the UK and abroad, therefore high-cost, uncompetitive products
- **Globalisation**: competition from overseas makers; purchase of equipment by other larger global producers; opening of biotech company Peen Pharma in Tredegar
- **High labour costs** compared with global competitors
- **Lifestyle changes**: emphasis on education and skills in the twenty-first century; environmental protection and sustainability in the new wetlands; the addition of an environmental resource centre
- **Boosterism**: publicity to create image of modernity represented by new activities yet keeping a sense of past Ebbw in the museum; a listed building

Exam tip

Always have examples to support every point you make. They can be extended examples for use in essays or brief examples to support a set of reasons or factors.

Decline in secondary employment in urban places

In 1980, the headline 'The murder of a town' was used to highlight the loss of 3,700 jobs in Consett when the steel works was closed, resulting in 36% unemployment. The following section provides further case studies illustrating the impact of decline on urban places.

Deindustrialisation is the decline in manufacturing industry. It can be caused by:

- a fall in the output of manufacturing
- the development of new improved products
- the growth of cheaper imports of the same products
- a drop in the number and share of employees in manufacturing as a result of factory closures, automation and lay-offs.

Not every industrial city has been able to remain successful. Detroit lost 58% of its population between 1950 and 2008 due to deindustrialisation, automation and foreign competition for the automobile industry. Declining population due to the decline in a city's port and shipbuilding industrial base has affected Liverpool and Glasgow.

Cheaper foreign competition from South Korea and Japan killed shipbuilding on the rivers Tyne and Wear. The loss of cotton textile and mining industries has particularly affected parts of Bolton, Rochdale, Oldham, Tameside and Wigan in Greater Manchester (Figure 10). In these places, 30% of neighbourhoods are counted among the 20% most deprived neighbourhoods in England. By 2011, only 9% of the UK workforce was employed in manufacturing.

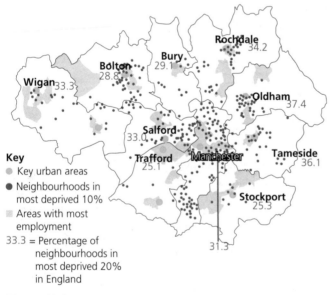

Key
- Key urban areas
- Neighbourhoods in most deprived 10%
- Areas with most employment

33.3 = Percentage of neighbourhoods in most deprived 20% in England

Figure 10 Employment and deprivation in Greater Manchester

Deprivation is the theme of the following section in this book.

Deindustrialisation affects places differently and results in different outcomes. Cities such as Stoke-on-Trent, Hull, Barnsley, Middlesbrough, Bolton and Blackburn have all been identified as struggling because new jobs are not replacing lost jobs. The qualified leave and the unqualified remain, which further reduces the attractiveness of the workforce to employers. Although many deindustrialised urban areas are deprived, they are surrounded by affluent rural areas. Hull is the ninth most deprived city in the UK, yet the surrounding East Riding is 208th.

Fieldwork

SSI, a Thai-owned company, closed the Redcar steelworks in 2015, resulting in the loss of 2,200 jobs. Employees who previously earned above the national average wage were now turning to Aldi and B&Q for jobs. Food banks now feed approximately 2,000 in nearby Middlesbrough. A supply firm has laid off 33% of its workforce. By using both personal and public accounts of the town before and after the closure it should be possible to demonstrate how a global firm has affected the lives of people in this place.

Summary

- The Clark Fisher Model provides a basic explanation of the changing balance of employment in developed economies over time.
- Kondratiev waves help to explain the relationships between technological change and the economic development of places and regions.
- The decline of the manufacturing industry in the UK and other developed economies is a consequence of factors emanating from both beyond the country and within the country/region.
- Deindustrialisation has been a significant outcome of the decline in manufacturing and has had a variable impact on places. It has given rise to inequalities both within and between towns and cities.
- Location quotients (LQs) measure the concentration of an activity in areas/regions.

■ Economic change and social inequalities in deindustrialised urban places

Consequences of the loss of traditional industries in urban areas

In 2016, Tata Steel, the Indian-owned steel-maker, announced 1,050 redundancies in the UK. The company employed 6,000 in Wales (4,000 in Port Talbot, where 1 in 4 people work in the steel industry) and 750 of these jobs are being declared redundant. Other Tata sites are in Llanwern (Newport), Llanelli, Shotton and Trostre. It has been estimated that the wages of Tata employees bring £200m to the Welsh economy. What are the effects of such announcements on the surrounding places?

Table 8 shows the broad consequences of deindustrialisation for selected cities with the lowest population growth between 2004 and 2014. Three Welsh cities have been added for comparative purposes. Each of the English places illustrates the direct and indirect effects on the economies and society. On every measure these former industrial cities fall well below the national average. Their contributions to the economy, attractiveness to new business, innovation as measured by patents and employment rates are below UK average. More residents have no qualifications and fewer have high-level qualifications. Only broadband connectivity is better than the national average. Wages and welfare payments provide a further indicator. All but Cardiff are what is classified as 'Low wage, high welfare' cities, whereas Cardiff, Exeter and Northampton are 'Low wage, low welfare'. In contrast, the row showing the best-achieving cities indicates that these are 'High wage, low welfare' cities.

Table 8 Selected characteristics of deindustrialised places with the lowest population change (after Centre for Cities, 2016)

Place	Population growth 2004–14	GVA* per person (£) 2014	% residents with high-level skills NVQ4 and higher 2014	% residents with no qualification 2014	New business start-ups per 10,000 population 2014	Patents per 10,000 population 2014	% employment rate 2014–15	% households with super-fast broad-band
Blackburn	0.4	40,300	23.5	14.6	43.3	3.4	63.8	61.2
Stoke	0.3	44,300	23.5	16.9	32.4	1.9	69.4	71.8
Hull	0.2	42,300	21.1	12.1	31.4	1.2	64.1	ND
Middlesbrough	0.1	45,100	28.6	10.3	40.89	1.1	66.9	73.5
Burnley	0.0	48,500	23.6	12.0	37.5	4	67.0	67.9
Sunderland	–0.1	44,900	23.2	10.9	30.2	1.1	63.9	75.3
Newport	5.9 (2001–11)	47,400	31.2	10.1	37.3	3.4	69.3	69.9
Swansea	5.8	41,800	31.8	11.8	32.4	2.6	68.5	70.5
Cardiff	13 (2002–13)	44,351	46.0	6.6	51.8	4.8	67.7	83.3
Lowest	—	Black-burn 40,300	Wakefield 20.7	Stoke 16.9	Belfast 28.8	Chatham 0.0	Liverpool 61.2	Barn-sley 60.2
Highest	Slough 1.8	London 73,000 Reading 70,900	Cambridge 61.4	Exeter 1.9	London 100.1 Northamp-ton 80.6	Cambridge 101.9	Aldershot 83.4	Luton 88.0
UK	0.7	53,700	35.8	9.0	54.3	3.6	72.9	63.4

* GVA measures the contribution to the economy of each individual.

Key

▨ Low age, high welfare cities

▨ High wage, low welfare cities

▨ Low wage, low welfare cities

▨ UK average

Knowledge check 6

Some places in Figure 11 occur in both high and low, e.g. Worthing, Luton and York. Why might this be so?

Figure 11 maps cities with the highest percentage of high earners and the greatest percentage of low earners in the workforce. Those places with low earners are mainly the cities of nineteenth-century *industrial* regions of England and Wales, whereas the high-earning cities are associated with employment diversity relating to the growth of the tertiary and quaternary sectors (*causality*, *inequality* and *difference*).

Deprivation

One social outcome of deindustrialisation is **multiple deprivation**. Deprivation is measured by the proportions of poor-quality housing, unskilled workforce, lack of employment opportunities, poor-quality housing, derelict sites and buildings, poor health, poor environmental quality, weak transport infrastructure and, often, contaminated land. These problems tend to be more visible in urban areas but they may also affect rural areas.

Figures 12 and 13 map the areas of greatest and least deprivation in Leicester and Wrexham. Similar maps can be found for almost every unitary authority in the country so that you can examine and understand the nature of the deprived localities in your own place. Figure 12 includes the rural area around Wrexham, whereas Figure 13 illustrates the immediate city of Leicester.

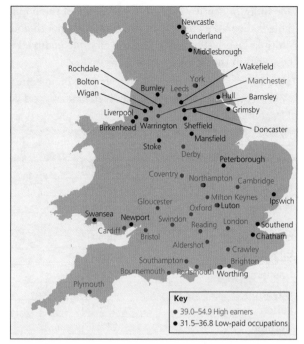

Figure 11 Cities with over 39% employed in high-paid occupations and over 31.5% employed in low-paid occupations in 2011

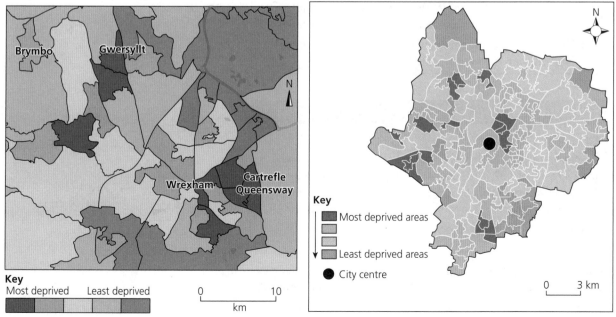

Figure 12 Deprivation in Wrexham

Figure 13 Deprivation in Leicester

One index of deprivation is the percentage of the population with no qualifications. Table 9 shows data for the 14 wards of Portsmouth and their ranking on the Index of Multiple Deprivation (IMD) for the city (*inequality*). Figure 14 shows the location of the wards in the city.

Table 9 Percentage of population over 16 with no educational qualifications, % overcrowded households, % terraced housing and IMD rank for the wards of Portsmouth

Ward name	% no qualifications (rank)	Overcrowding % households (rank)	% terraced accommodation (rank)	IMD rank (Figure 14)
Charles Dickens	31.5 (2)	8.8 (1)	14.2 (14)	1
Paulsgrove	32.8 (1)	5.0 (7)	42.1 (7)	2
Nelson	27.8 (3)	6.1 (4)	63.3 (5)	3
Fratton	21.7 (6)	6.2 (3)	71.7 (2)	4
St Thomas	15.9 (12)	7.9 (2)	22.2 (12)	5
St Jude	13.3 (13)	5.6 (5)	23.0 (11)	6
Cosham	25.1 (4)	4.2 (8)	38.6 (9)	7
Hilsea	23.2 (5)	3.8 (9)	40.5 (8)	8
Milton	19.4 (8)	3.5 (10)	70.7 (3)	9
Baffins	21.5 (7)	3.1 (13)	61.9 (6)	10
Eastney and Craneswater	16.8 (11)	3.2 (11.5)	38.4 (10)	11
Central Southsea	11.6 (14)	5.4 (6)	72.0 (1)	12
Copnor	19.2 (9)	3.2 (11.5)	66.3 (4)	13
Drayton and Farlington	17.9 (10)	1.5 (14)	18.8 (13)	14

Self-study task

Statistical 1

1 Calculate the mode, arithmetic mean or average and median for the data for those wards with no qualifications.

2 Calculate the standard deviation from the mean and the deviation from the median data in column 1.

Self-study task

Statistical 2

A Spearman rank test (Rs) was carried out on columns 2 and 4. It gave a result of 0.82. What does this tell you? A test on columns 3 and 4 gave a result of −0.19. What does this result indicate? Now perform a Spearman rank test on columns 2 and 3.

The answers can be found on page 115.

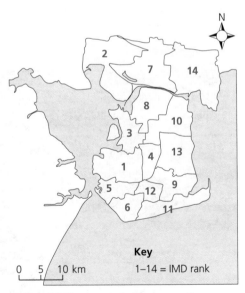

Figure 14 The wards in Portsmouth

Many areas of deprivation suffer from territorial stigmatisation, where an area is typecast because of its reputation and perceived changes to the population mix of its neighbourhoods (*identity*). In some cases, these areas may be perceived as ghettos due to the ethnic mix of the people living there. The term 'ghetto' comes from Renaissance

Venice, where the Jewish population was forced to live in a separate district. Ghettoes enable the dominant social groups to isolate a community in a distinct, identifiable area.

In Europe, it has been partly a consequence of deindustrialisation that some of these areas have been described as 'decomposing steadily'. St Pauls, Bristol is a case in point; close to the city centre, partly destroyed by bombing and rebuilt with social housing, together with some older squares and terraces, it became an area of Afro-Caribbean immigrants intermixed with lower paid and unemployed people. How did the place become stigmatised? The area was associated with riots in 1980, drugs and an alternative culture (*causality*). Some taxi drivers will still not enter St Pauls at night. These views dominate efforts to instigate neighbourhood renewal, while residents themselves are suspicious of those groups involved in renewal because they come from outside, and appear to focus on physical infrastructure rather than issues of employment and inequality.

Social exclusion

Social exclusion is being outside of or marginalised from mainstream society, its resources and the opportunities provided by them. It often involves **stigma**, or severe disapproval of an individual or group. It can be multidimensional because it can be a result of class, gender, race, ethnicity, sexuality and/or age (*difference*). Homeless people are an excluded group, some of whom may be in the predicament due to loss of employment. They are then viewed as unproductive and disaffiliated. They are part of the **Cycle of Deprivation**, a sequence of events that disadvantaged people experience in which one problem, e.g. lack of work, leads to other problems and so makes things worse. Socially excluded individuals tend to drift towards the city centres, which are seen to have the best environments and public spaces for their lifestyles. The reaction is to 'design out' the problematic activities and introduce cultures of respect. Exclusion may not reach these levels but elements of the process can be seen in:

- stigmatisation of the people living on council estates with high unemployment, often referred to as 'shirkers' or 'benefits cheats'
- neighbourhoods regarded as 'no-go areas' because of petty criminality and mental health issues
- the development of red light districts
- costs of rental housing and the council house right-to-buy policy.

A consequence of exclusion is the creation of socioeconomic areas in settlements depending on people's ability to pay, earning power, social status and, in the past, zoning (*causality*).

Pollution levels and deindustrialisation

In 2013, fuel burning accounted for 83% of pollution. Closure of heavy industries such as steel works and coal-fired power stations has reduced the amount of sulphur dioxide (SO_2) in the air. SO_2 emissions have declined to 7% of their 1970 levels. Between 1970 and 2013 industrial combustion emissions fell by 94%. Most of the decrease took place between 1970 and 1985 with the decline in energy-intensive iron and steel, and other heavy industries. There has been also been a decline in the use of coal and fuel oil in favour of natural gas in power generation. To meet the Gothenburg Protocol target in 2020, the UK will have to further cut emissions by 26%. If you are interested in the effects of the many pollutants on people, go to www.naei.defra.gov.uk/overview/pollutants?pollutant_id=8.

Consequences of the loss of primary industries in rural areas

The average age of a farmer in the UK is 59. The average age is rising because older farmers do not retire. The challenges are great for primary industries, especially in the more remote areas. In Wales, 60% of its 20,000 km² is agricultural and 9.5% forested. The population densities are low, the average farm size is small (59ha) and accessibility is by narrow roads. ICT and broadband connectivity is poor. It is difficult to provide services when there are few settlements that can be hubs to serve a wide area. Farms lack a skilled workforce so that much of the Rural Development Planning money is being invested in up-skilling 13,000 farmers. Out-migration of the young in order to gain qualifications elsewhere leaves a young population with low-level qualifications and high unemployment; 6.9% in rural areas are unemployed (*risk*).

The **Welsh Index of Multiple Deprivation (WIMD)** has identified 389 of the most deprived areas in Wales. The components of the index are shown in Figure 15. Each domain contains further indicators and those for Access to Services are given. In many rural areas, the *threshold* for these services is not reached.

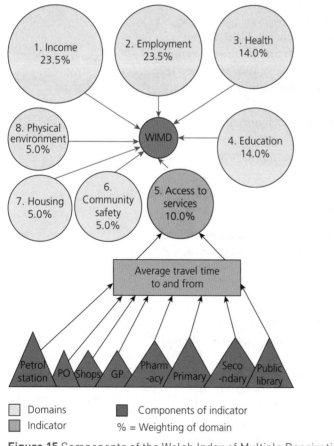

Figure 15 Components of the Welsh Index of Multiple Deprivation (WIMD)

Figure 16 maps deprivation in Wales in 2014. There are few deprivation hot spots in rural Wales. They tend to be small towns (Newtown), the most remote mountainous areas and the extreme periphery (Llyn Peninsula). Only 2% of the most deprived areas in Wales are rural but 18% of the most deprived live in rural areas. Deprivation is not necessarily concentrated and local and regional government can miss it, because individual cases get lost, since the data is based on extensive statistical areas.

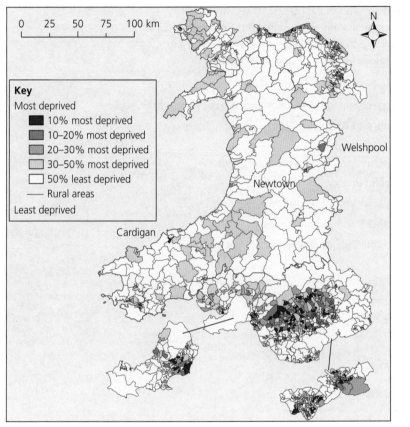

Figure 16 The Welsh Index of Multiple Deprivation (after the Welsh Government)

Government policies in deindustrialised places

This is an ever-changing topic, as governments at all levels, from international to local, continuously alter policies.

International European Structural and Investment Funds 2014–20

Regional policy is delivered through three main funds: the European Regional Development Fund (ERDF), the Cohesion Fund (CF) and the European Social Fund (ESF). Together with the European Agricultural Fund for Rural Development (EAFRD) and the European Maritime and Fisheries Fund (EMFF), they make up the European Structural and Investment (ESI) Funds. All of these programmes are now under one umbrella: **The Growth Programme**.

The European Regional Development Fund

The European Regional Development Fund (ERDF) commenced operation in 1975. Its main objective is to support projects and activities that reduce the economic disparity within the member states of the EU. It financially aids projects that stimulate economic development and increase employment by supporting inward investment and retraining in the poorest regions. It helps to preserve natural environments in order to improve the quality of life of residents and make regions more attractive to tourists and investors. Infrastructural investments and educational retraining schemes are supported and there is help to promote regional development and reduce the gap between the wealthiest and the poorest regions (*adaptation* and *mitigation*).

The priorities are:

1 Strengthening research, technological development and innovation (tertiary growth)

2 Enhancing information, communication and technology (tertiary and quaternary growth)

3 Enhancing the competitiveness of small and medium-sized enterprises

4 Supporting the shift towards a low carbon economy

5 Promoting climate change adaptation, risk prevention and management

6 Preserving and protecting the environment and promoting resource efficiency

7 Promoting sustainable transport and removing bottlenecks in key network infrastructures

8 Promoting social inclusion, and combating poverty and any discrimination

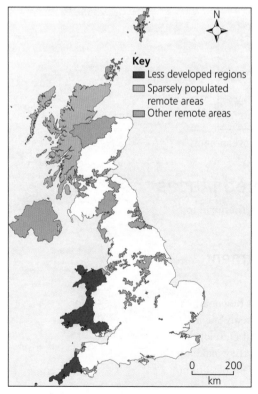

Figure 17 The assisted areas in the UK

There are three types of regional support in the UK:

1 **More developed areas:** covers most of England, designed to reduce economic, environmental and social problems in urban areas, with a special focus on sustainable urban development.

2 **Areas that are naturally disadvantaged by remoteness/mountains and are sparsely populated:** the most peripheral areas also benefit from specific assistance from the ERDF to address possible disadvantages due to their remoteness, such as the Scottish Highlands and Islands.

3 **Less developed regions:** only one region in England falls into this category, Cornwall and the Isles of Scilly, while the Welsh regions are West Wales and the Valleys.

Fieldwork

Is there an ERDF project in your area — probably the first type of support? If so, examine what it aims to do and evaluate its success. Does it provide jobs or merely replace jobs, and does it improve the environment and attract visitors? In other words, who is gaining and who is losing? What effect will leaving the EU have on this project?

The European Social Fund

The European Social Fund (ESF) aims to:

- tackle poverty and social exclusion by increasing employment and helping people to access sustainable employment
- invest in skills and improve the diversity of the workforce
- invest in our young people with the necessary skills for a challenging knowledge-based economy

All of these are *mitigation*.

To be successful the programme aims to:

- reduce poverty
- increase skills levels of the workforce, and reduce the number of people with no skills or basic skills
- increase youth employment and attainment
- reduce inequalities in the labour market among women and recognise other disadvantaged groups

All involve *adaptation*, *risk* and *mitigation*.

National Funding: Enterprise Zones

Figure 18 shows the location of the **Enterprise Zones (EZs)** in England (24) and Wales (7). There are 15 EZs in Scotland. EZs are now a part of the **Local Enterprise Partnership (LEP)** programme. Enterprise Zones in urban areas have been successful ever since they were established in the 1980s. Figure 19 shows the distribution of employment in Swansea in 2013. The former EZ Swansea 1 was the location for 25% of new private sector jobs in the city, more than in the city centre (18%).

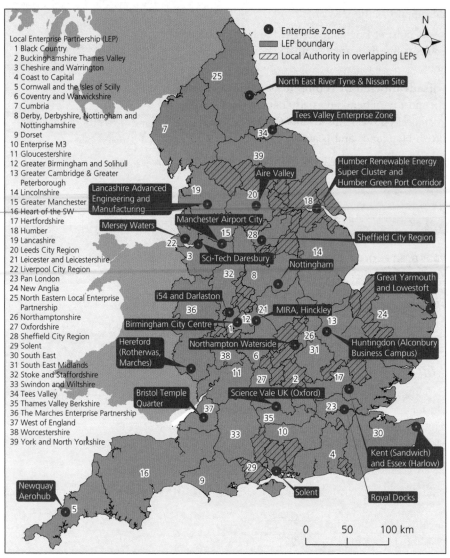

Figure 18 Enterprise Zones and Local Enterprise Partnerships in England

Within the map:

Local Enterprise Partnership (LEP)
1 Black Country
2 Buckinghamshire Thames Valley
3 Cheshire and Warrington
4 Coast to Capital
5 Cornwall and the Isles of Scilly
6 Coventry and Warwickshire
7 Cumbria
8 Derby, Derbyshire, Nottingham and Nottinghamshire
9 Dorset
10 Enterprise M3
11 Gloucestershire
12 Greater Birmingham and Solihull
13 Greater Cambridge & Greater Peterborough
14 Lincolnshire
15 Greater Manchester
16 Heart of the SW
17 Hertfordshire
18 Humber
19 Lancashire
20 Leeds City Region
21 Leicester and Leicestershire
22 Liverpool City Region
23 Pan London
24 New Anglia
25 North Eastern Local Enterprise Partnership
26 Northamptonshire
27 Oxfordshire
28 Sheffield City Region
29 Solent
30 South East
31 South East Midlands
32 Stoke and Staffordshire
33 Swindon and Wiltshire
34 Tees Valley
35 Thames Valley Berkshire
36 The Marches Enterprise Partnership
37 West of England
38 Worcestershire
39 York and North Yorkshire

Legend:
● Enterprise Zones
▢ LEP boundary
▨ Local Authority in overlapping LEPs

Labels: North East River Tyne & Nissan Site; Tees Valley Enterprise Zone; Humber Renewable Energy Super Cluster and Humber Green Port Corridor; Aire Valley; Lancashire Advanced Engineering and Manufacturing; Mersey Waters; Manchester Airport City; Sheffield City Region; Sci-Tech Daresbury; Nottingham; Great Yarmouth and Lowestoft; i54 and Darlaston; MIRA, Hinckley; Birmingham City Centre; Hereford (Rotherwas, Marches); Northampton Waterside; Huntingdon (Alconbury Business Campus); Science Vale UK (Oxford); Bristol Temple Quarter; Kent (Sandwich) and Essex (Harlow); Newquay Aerohub; Solent; Royal Docks

Scale: 0 50 100 km

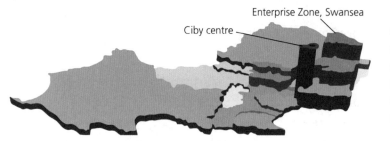

Figure 19 Employment change in Swansea 2013

Labels: Enterprise Zone, Swansea; Ciby centre

Legend:
● 6,001–11,500
● 4,001–6,000
● 2,001–4,000
● 901–2,000
● 401–900
● 231–400

Local Enterprise Partnerships

Local Enterprise Partnerships (LEPs) are part of the current Enterprise Zone (EZ) policy in the UK. Solent LEP (Figure 20) not only focuses on the six major areas

---

Knowledge check 7

What are the advantages and disadvantages of portraying the data in Figure 19?

Exam tip

You must be able to evaluate the merits and drawbacks of every form of data portrayal geographers use.

Fieldwork

Examine the past, present and proposed land uses in an Enterprise Zone. The website http://businesswales.gov.wales/enterprise zones/ provides a good starting point as a secondary source with which to start your work.

within the LEP — one of which, Welbourne, is a greenfield site — but also improving aspects of the more deprived parts of the LEP.

Community Grants are being used to assist wards with high levels of unemployment and poor social cohesion. There are 16 wards on the Isle of Wight and four wards in Havant, all of which are located on a former council overspill estate built in the 1950s, which are eligible for funding.

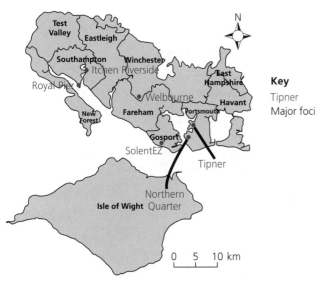

Figure 20 The Solent LEP, Solent EZ and its six brownfield regeneration sites

Fieldwork

If there is a ward near you that has high levels of unemployment, examine the ward to assess its identity, representation and what steps are being taken to mitigate social cohesion.

Foreign Direct Investment

Foreign Direct Investment (FDI) is an investment made by a company based in one country, into a company based in another country. Most FDI takes the form of investment by large multinational companies (MNCs). Economies with skilled workforces and good growth prospects tend to attract larger amounts of FDI. 1,988 FDI projects generated 84,000 jobs in the UK in 2014–15:

1 It can take the form of major MNC investments, such as Toyota at Burleston, Nissan at Sunderland, Lockheed Martin Space in Harwell and BMW/Rolls Royce most recently in Bognor (interdependence).

2 It can also occur in the built environment, such as The Shard, Malaysian investment in the Battersea redevelopment and UAE interests in the regeneration of East Manchester (Etihad Stadium). Not all schemes are new because some FDI comes through the takeover of existing companies. Masdar from the UAE is now the largest wind-farm operator in the UK. Hong Kong investors now own the port of Felixstowe.

3   FDI also attracts tertiary and quaternary industries (pages 46–65). Cray Computers (Seattle) opened their first office outside the USA in Bristol. A third of FDI projects in 2015 were in the quaternary sector.

FDI investments have often been associated with government policies to regenerate places or areas, as is the case with Nissan in the North East. The Welsh government assisted in the expansion of R&D facilities for an Israeli IT company in Newport. However, many MNCs still prefer to invest in successful places (*identity*).

Fieldwork

Select an FDI investment and assess its impact on the environment and the people who live close to the investment. Who is gaining from it and who is losing due to the investment?

Summary

- Deindustrialisation affects the economic diversity of places, which has a range of social effects, especially deprivation.
- Multiple deprivation will vary between and within places/regions. It can be statistically analysed using secondary sources from the census.
- Rural areas have also lost employment in traditional primary industries.
- Governments at the international, national and local levels have policies to mitigate the loss of employment and to create the opportunities for new employment.

■ The service economy (tertiary) and its social and economic impacts

In 2011, 81% of the working population of the UK was employed in the service sector (including quaternary — pages 58–65) compared with 76% in 2001. 92% of working women are employed in the sector and 71% of men. The service and quaternary economies are the main employers in UK settlements.

Factors that promote service sector growth

The tertiary or service sector grew to support the manufacturing sector, as industrialists needed to finance growth, buy raw materials and market their products. It also grew as workers became more prosperous and they, like the companies they worked for, required banks, insurance and lawyers. In order to ensure maximum contact with their clients and rapid communication of ideas these services were initially located in city centres. Many cities have legal districts close to the law courts. Government also grew at both national and local level, often leading to the construction of large town halls and administrative districts that reflected the wealth of the city and its region (e.g. Cathays Park, Cardiff) (*causality* and *time*). Firms that sell knowledge, such as finance, law and marketing, benefit from proximity because they can gain from the exchange of knowledge when they are clustered.

Technology

Technological inventions enhanced clustering of office buildings in central business districts (CBDs) and city centres:

- The steel framed skyscraper, first built in Chicago in 1884, enabled vertical development, as did the invention of the electric lift (1880) and electric escalator (1892).
- The telephone (patented in 1876) enabled quicker communication. The telegraph (1844), which allowed for long-distance communications, was its forerunner but not the key factor in tertiary sector development. However, the first telegraph cable across the Atlantic (1866) can be seen as a forerunner of the globalisation of communications.
- Electric power lay behind the late nineteenth-century developments in communication and movement of people.
- Transport developments and especially the building of tramways, and, in the larger cities, underground lines, enabled the growing labour force to commute to work over greater distances (*causality*).

Prosperity

Prosperity and affluence have also encouraged the growth of the service sector; people want to invest and bank their wealth, insure their property and possessions, purchase goods and have improved leisure time. More disposable income has led to the growth of leisure industries (*recreation* and *tourism*) including the rise of travel agencies (*causality, place, time*).

Transport and communication

Changing transport technologies have enabled retailing, offices and leisure industries to disperse beyond the city centre, across urban areas. Rail travel gave rise to the growth of seaside resorts in the nineteenth century, aided by social developments such as mandatory annual holidays. The developments in aircraft technologies have led to overseas package tourism and increasingly long-distance tourism and ecotourism (*causality, difference, place*).

Changing communication technologies are also altering the distribution of the service economy. Online booking has largely replaced travel agencies. Hotels and conference centres have become key functions for business life and tourism in most major cities, e.g. Bournemouth International Centre (BIC) and Venue Cymru in Llandudno.

Retailing, commercial and entertainment expansion in some central areas

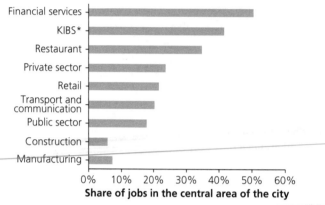

* Knowledge Intensive Business Services

Figure 21 The concentration of jobs in central areas of cities in 2011

Self-study task

Is the concentration of jobs shown in Figure 21 reflected in the town or city that you have studied? Can you explain why your place may be different?

Table 10 The city centre timeline

Nineteenth century	Movement into cities during Industrial Revolution	URBANISATION
Early twentieth century	Business agglomerations and HQs concentrated in big city centres	AGGLOMERATION
1930s	Rapid suburban growth; car ownership rising	
1940s	Second World War bomb damage to centres — reconstruction necessary	
1950s–60s	Rising car ownership; abandonment of inner city for suburbs and estates	
1960s–70s	Large-scale rebuilding, slum clearance, large commercial buildings; affluence rising	
1960s–80s	Decline of manufacturing and deterioration of industrial cities; office development restricted in London and spreads to other cities	
1970s and 80s	Early gentrification in London (Notting Hill, Islington, Fulham); increasing car dependence; urban motorway schemes halted	DECENTRALISATION
1980s	Fewer restrictions on commercial space outside of town centres; retail parks	
1980–2000	Expansion of tertiary economy and demand for office space	
1980s–90s	Urban regeneration — increase in retail, office and leisure space in CBD	
1990s	Growing use of ICT and telephonic technologies	
1990–2000	Out-of-town development restricted; congestion as a result of more car travel; reurbanisation commences	REURBANISATION
2008–2014	Recession, retail vacancies rise; internet shopping affects retailing	

City centres are the location of 72% of all highly skilled jobs and are 21% more productive than non-urban areas. Graduates, attracted to the concentration of knowledge-based jobs, take half of the jobs in city centres. A central business district (CBD) is a more confined area associated with offices, administration and retail, whereas the Central Area includes other land uses, such as residential and leisure. Nearly all large cities have seen job growth, although many medium-sized urban areas have not.

Benefits of city centre locations

1 **Agglomeration** and **proximity** are the prime benefits of a city centre location for business and retailing (Figure 22). The centre shares the infrastructure (roads, railways) of the entire city. The urban area has a large pool of workers that employers can tap into. The centre is the area where ideas and information can be sold and exchanged, much by face-to-face contact, which is the traditional method and is still important today (e.g. in clubs such as Soho House in London). This is known as **knowledge spillover**. Finance, law and marketing are major gainers in many city centres.

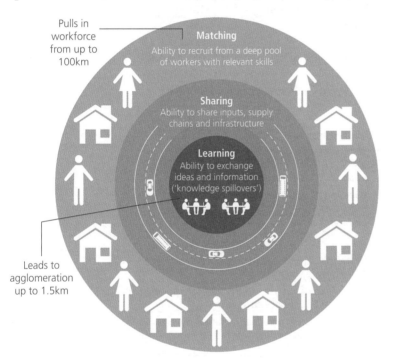

Pulls in workforce from up to 100km

Leads to agglomeration up to 1.5km

Matching
Ability to recruit from a deep pool of workers with relevant skills

Sharing
Ability to share inputs, supply chains and infrastructure

Learning
Ability to exchange ideas and information ('knowledge spillovers')

Figure 22 The benefits of agglomeration

2 **Accessibility** allows for better shopping locations for lower-income groups because there is more choice and chances to compare. Out-of-town employment locations have fewer public transport connections and are therefore less accessible for the low paid.

3 **Highly qualified labour pools** attract the skilled service companies, who in turn attract skilled workers; the share of graduates in Cambridge (36%), London (32%), Oxford (31%) and Reading (28%) in 2011 explains why these cities attract the highly skilled economic activities to their centres and nearby locations (*causality* and *difference*).

Is retailing declining in city/town centres and, if so, why?

Retailing can only succeed if there are people who live and work in the city centre. The more retailing moves out-of-town, the fewer people will shop in the city centre. In 2013, 1 in 8 shops in the UK was vacant. Table 11 shows the shops that are leaving town centres (fallers) and those that are on the increase (risers). Those that are opening may be linked to a rise in low salaries and the needs of the disadvantaged.

Table 11 Change in number of shops in 500 British town centres, 2012 (*The Grimsey Review*)

Risers	Units	Fallers	Units
Charity shops	+174	Women's clothing	−264
Pawnbrokers	+128	Recruitment agencies	−210
Convenience stores	+113	Computer games	−187
Cheque cashing	+64	Card and poster shops	−184
Nail bars	+106	Toy shops	−119

Shops are increasingly becoming showrooms for browsing, making way for online and delivered-direct or 'click and collect' purchases. Table 12 lists some of the advantages and disadvantages of physical shopping. The reverse could easily apply to those of internet shopping.

Table 12 Physical shopping advantages and disadvantages

Advantages of physical shopping	Disadvantages of physical shopping
More pleasant and social	Opening hours are often limited
Can make unexpected, impulse purchases	Getting to and from shops, congestion and cost
Shopping as leisure — coffee bars	Parking and transport costs high
Individual service from approachable retailers	Less easy to compare prices in different shops
Direct possession and use	Pushy sales people
Feeling of reliability because of ability to make comparisons	More expensive due to the cost of space to store and display goods
Perceived as being more versatile because products can be compared	Lack of background information on products and services, which the internet can provide

Table 13 illustrates a selection of e-commerce sales.

Table 13 Online/e-commerce sales 2015

Retail type	% purchased online	Internet sales as % of all internet sales by value	Retail type	% purchased online	Internet sales as % of all internet sales by value
Electronics	49	29.0	Cosmetics	No data	2.3
Fashion	19	28.6	Books	45	1.5
Grocery	6	19.9	Music products	42	1.3
Furniture	No data	2.7	—	—	—

The financial failure of retailers also impacts city centres. In 2016, both BHS and Austin Reed were placed in administration. Closed frontages, especially in larger stores, can alter the image of a high street. The replacement retail outlet might not return the street to its former image, causing the attractiveness of certain streets/

Knowledge check 8

Describe and explain the data in Table 13.

centres to decline further. The loss of jobs may reduce the importance of a town centre as a place of work and tourism (*adaptation*, *attachment*, *difference* and *resilience*).

Nearest neighbour analysis of shops clustering in a centre

On a plan of the shopping area or centre onto which you have mapped the different types of shop (a Goad Plan will be a useful start, although you must check its accuracy)

1 measure the distance between each retail type (e.g. shoe shops, mobile phone shops, jewellers), and its nearest neighbour
2 tabulate the nearest distances for each retail type
3 find the mean distance between each of the pairs of nearest neighbours
4 measure the total area of the centre that you are studying
   Note: use the same unit of measurement (e.g. metres). It is best to measure within a rectangle covering the area where you wish to measure clustering.
5 calculate using the formula:

$$R_n = \frac{\dot{D}}{0.5(1/\sqrt{(A/N)})}$$

- R_n is the description of the distribution
- $\dot{D}$ is the mean distance between the neighbours
- A is the area being studied
- N is the number of points.

The results that you obtain will always range between 0 and 2.15. If all shoe shops were perfectly clustered (near/next to each other in a small area), R_n would be 0 and if randomly distributed, R_n would be 2.25. A figure of 1.9 would suggest some regularity to the distribution of that retail type.

Gentrification and associated social changes in central urban places experiencing reurbanisation

Global wealth is affecting local change. **Gentrification** is the consequence of economic and social change in central urban places. The term is used to define the concentration of high and ultra-high net worth individuals in the centre of major world cities (London, New York, Tokyo). London's ultra-high wealth individuals had an average property portfolio of US$28m in 2014. The reasons why many of these people invest in Central London are:

- property investment gives high returns due to inflation
- demand for accommodation; the UK is a safe place for investment
- they wish to have a home for their globalised lifestyle.

Gentrification is associated with the service economy and reurbanisation. It sees highly educated professional, creative, technical and managerial workers replace industrial workers. Property developers with financial backing also convert older industrial buildings into apartments in these areas (*causality*, *adaptation*, *risk* and *resilience*).

- Wapping, London was the first area in the city in which waterside warehouses were converted into apartments. This trend has spread to other areas of London where former industrial buildings have been abandoned.

Exam tip for fieldwork

When describing a city centre, do describe the upper storeys of buildings, which give a better impression of the centre in the past. Shop fronts are recent additions, yet the buildings they are in are often much older.

Fieldwork

Complete an analysis of the clustering of retailing using nearest neighbour analysis. This could have a historical dimension.

Fieldwork

Examine the distribution of vacant space in and around a CBD. What used to be there and why are the spaces now vacant/derelict? What types of business do people living in the town wish to see taking up these vacant lots, in order to be more representative of their town?

- More recently, the clearance of brownfield sites such as Battersea Power Station and areas of poor-quality buildings around it are being developed into luxury high-rise apartments.
- In areas such as Shoreditch and Hoxton, former nineteenth-century working class residential districts, houses are being converted to house the highly paid city employees. The 1902 Brune Street Soup Kitchen for the Jewish Poor has been converted into luxury flats. Edward England Wharf in Cardiff is a former potato factory that is being converted into apartments. Even in rural places, such as Arundel, the nineteenth-century Poor House has been converted to flats.

Knowledge check 9

Gentrification is occurring in many cities (Leeds, Liverpool, Newcastle, Cardiff, etc.). What types of buildings are being converted? What is the effect on the social geography of the city?

Between 1971 and 1991 the number of people living in the centre of UK cities declined. However, since 1991, the population in city centres has risen, and in fact doubled between 2001 and 2011. The bigger the city, the faster the growth has been. What are the drivers of the dominance of reurbanisation?

- **Building of flats and apartments:** more flats built in Central Manchester between 2001 and 2011 than in the whole of London.
- **Permitted development rights:** allow developers to convert offices to residential use in those areas where demand for residences is high.
- **Rapid population increase:** in Manchester and Sheffield, the city centre population grew by 198% and 111% respectively between 2001 and 2011.
- **Increase in student numbers at universities located in city centres:** 39% of university students in Manchester live in the city centre.
- **Increase in 25–34-year-old professionals in highly skilled jobs:** in larger cities they are more likely to be single graduates; in smaller cities they are family members often commuting into the city to work.
- **People live and work in the centre:** 39% of Central Manchester's population also works in the city centre.
- **Leisure and cultural facilities:** usually dependent on the young, educated population.
- **Cost of living:** in less successful twenty-first-century towns, such as Doncaster, Newport and Worthing, it is cheaper to live in the city centre.

A 2015 survey highlighting the reasons why people lived in the centres of Manchester and Brighton is summarised in Table 14 (*identity, meaning* and *representation*).

Table 14 Reasons for people living in the centres of Brighton and Manchester (percentage of those surveyed who mentioned reason)

Brighton	Reason	Manchester
30%	Close to restaurants, leisure — the centre as a central entertainment district	60%
15%	Close to workplace	40%
28%	Public transport	32%
15%	Type of housing available	5%
23%	Cost of housing	26%
4%	I grew up here	1%

These people are the gentrifiers who work long hours and need to live close to their work. They also want the cultural and entertainment opportunities that a city centre provides.

Fieldwork

Examine the types of gentrification in a place either where you live or that you can study.

The complexity of the changing service economy

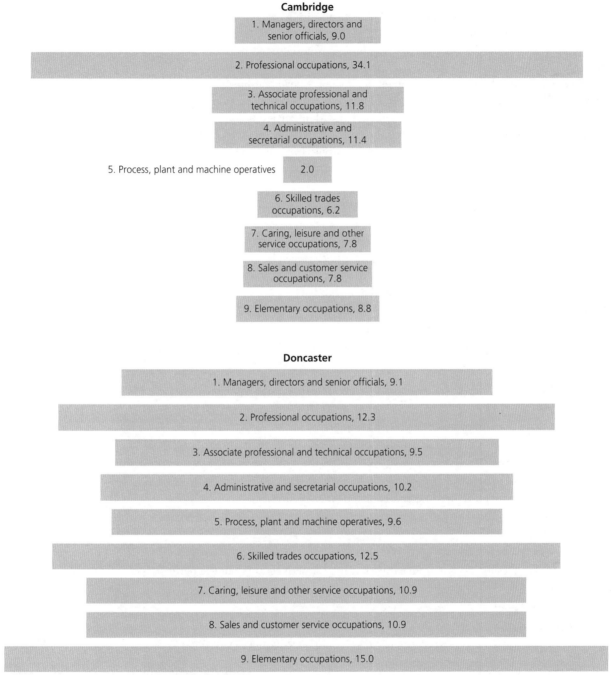

Cambridge

1. Managers, directors and senior officials, 9.0

2. Professional occupations, 34.1

3. Associate professional and technical occupations, 11.8

4. Administrative and secretarial occupations, 11.4

5. Process, plant and machine operatives 2.0

6. Skilled trades occupations, 6.2

7. Caring, leisure and other service occupations, 7.8

8. Sales and customer service occupations, 7.8

9. Elementary occupations, 8.8

Doncaster

1. Managers, directors and senior officials, 9.1

2. Professional occupations, 12.3

3. Associate professional and technical occupations, 9.5

4. Administrative and secretarial occupations, 10.2

5. Process, plant and machine operatives, 9.6

6. Skilled trades occupations, 12.5

7. Caring, leisure and other service occupations, 10.9

8. Sales and customer service occupations, 10.9

9. Elementary occupations, 15.0

Figure 23 Employment by occupation groups in Cambridge and Doncaster 2011

All urban areas grow and decline as a result of the changing social and economic forces over time. The service economy has resulted in population growth and changing lifestyles in all urban areas, but mainly in the southeast of the UK. Between

1971 and 2009, population growth in towns and cities was rapid (Milton Keynes 253%, Telford 67%, Crawley 29%, Cambridge 47%, Reading 34%).

On the other hand, during the same period, deindustrialising urban areas were losing people and economic activity (Liverpool −19%, Tyneside −10%, Stoke-on-Trent −4%, Burnley −3%). Demand for space and for new buildings in these places is low and, in the core, dwellings may be vacant/derelict. In declining cities there are attempts to improve the quality of the built environment and people's neighbourhoods through **remediation** (clearing derelict sites), which aims to bring the land back into use as offices, business parks, leisure, tourism and housing. Many such top-down schemes have limited success and have not created the anticipated number of jobs. They have come to depend on local government financing (e.g. Barnsley Gateway) because there is little demand for commercial property.

Furthermore, because the emphasis is mainly on commercial regeneration, the effect on people has been largely negative. 'The starting point for any serious urban policy is to recognise that the objective should be to enrich and empower the lives of people, no matter where they live' (Ed Glaeser 2008). For some cities, 'smart decline' and creating more green space would be better options (*difference* and *mitigation*).

Functions: why, where and examples

The growth of the service economy over the past 50 years has seen a wider variety of locations selected and occupied than ever before.

Retailing (out-of-town)

- Rise of superstores, e.g. Sainsbury's, Tesco
- DIY boom: either purpose-built or in converted industrial units, e.g. Homebase, IKEA
- Electrical and electronic goods, e.g. Dixon Group
- Furniture and homeware, e.g. Furniture Village, DFS, John Lewis
- Clothing, e.g. Next
- Combined sites to increase customer flow, often adjacent to major junctions, e.g. M&S and Sainsbury's, Hedge End Southampton (*interdependence*)
- Outlet stores, e.g. Bicester Village, Bridgend Designer Outlet, Wales; Cheshire Oaks Designer Outlet
- Retail-attached service stations and service areas on motorways, e.g. M&S, Waitrose
- Industrial estates: many date from earlier in the twentieth century but the newer industries are service orientated, replacing small former industrial units, e.g. double glazing, car wash

Retailing (city centre)

- City centre regeneration, e.g. WestQuay, Southampton; St David's Dewy Sant, Cardiff; Westfield London, Hammersmith.
- Creating a new city centre, e.g. Westfield Valley Fair Mall in San José, California has a new open-air shopping and leisure (hotels and restaurants) street, Santana Row, leading from it which creates a more traditional image of a city centre (*interdependence*)
- Regeneration of redundant industrial space, e.g. Gunwharf Quays, Portsmouth

- New convenience stores, renovated pubs, corner shops within the inner suburbs, e.g. SPAR, Tesco Express
- Car showrooms on routes into city/urban area, e.g. BMW, Audi
- Specialist shops in small towns, e.g. fashion, cheese, booksellers, antiques
- Charity shops, loan shops, betting shops, usually in smaller centres and streets leading to a centre
- Internet, but location free: will affect size of stores for some retailers

Offices

- Suburban clusters, e.g. Canary Wharf, London
- Barn conversions to form small office parks in rural areas (*resilience*)
- Office parks, e.g. on the reclaimed Port Solent, Portsmouth (began when IBM's offices were decentralised from London) (*space*)
- University developed science parks, e.g. Cambridge, Southampton, Stanford Research Park, San José, California (*interdependence*)

Leisure

- Leisure quarter in UK city centres often in converted buildings
- Restaurants taking over from former uses, e.g. Jamie's Cambridge and Zizi, Cardiff in former banks (*adaptation, resilience*)
- Multiplex cinemas both on CBD fringe and out-of-town, often in combination with retail developments (*interdependence*)
- Multi-purpose leisure centres, e.g. Fleming Park Eastleigh.
- Visitor centres, museums and galleries in converted or regenerated buildings, e.g. San Francisco Museum of Modern Art (SFMOMA) (*adaptation*)
- Hotels, near entry points to city and on motorways, e.g. Premier Inn, Ibis
- Hotels as part of regeneration, e.g. St David's Hotel, Cardiff Bay; Ghirardelli Hotel, San Francisco, in a former chocolate factory (*adaptation*)
- Conference centres, e.g. BIC and International Convention Centre (ICC) Birmingham, Santa Clara Convention Centre, California (*globalisation*)
- Exhibition centres out-of-town, e.g. National Exhibition Centre (NEC) Birmingham; Excel London; San Matteo Event Centre, California (*globalisation* of products and activities)
- Stadia as concert venues, e.g. Wembley, Principality Stadium (formerly Millennium Stadium) Cardiff; Levi Stadium, Santa Clara, California (*globalisation* of sports and stadium concerts)

All of these developments do have **risks**. Can you relate the key concepts to all of the bullets above? (There are several examples already included as a guide.)

How has central city retailing changed? Not all of the reasons apply everywhere but examine how they apply to your home town (*difference, adaptation* and *sustainability*):

- More specialisation resulting from new products such as mobile phones
- New retailers replacing those that left, e.g. Primark in old Woolworths stores
- New large-scale retail developments with anchor stores such as John Lewis, St David's, Cardiff and Grand Central, Birmingham
- Lower turnover of shops on side streets due to their lack of visibility or footfall
- Greater affluence, designer brands that sometimes cluster, e.g. The Hayes, Cardiff

> **Exam tip**
>
> Always try to have a bank of examples from beyond the UK to demonstrate your breadth of knowledge. The non-UK examples above are all from the Silicon Valley area of California, a contrasting place.

- New technologies, e.g. 'click and collect'
- Rising car ownership, but costs of parking and congestion can deter visitors
- In the less frequented and peripheral streets, the rise of betting shops/casinos, charity shops and loan/pawn shops. These can take over the heart of some less prosperous towns.

Impacts of tertiarisation on employment

The rise of the service-based economy has been accompanied by the growth of professional, managerial, technical and creative employment of highly educated and highly paid persons.

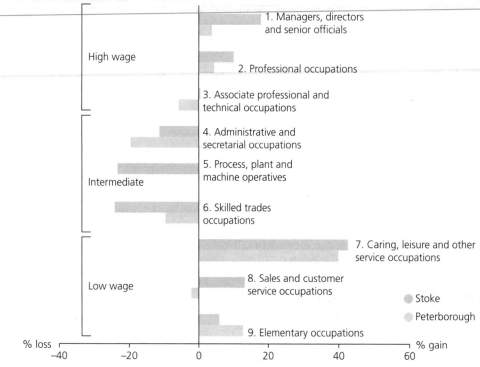

Figure 24 Changing occupational structure in Peterborough and Stoke-on-Trent 2011

Knowledge check 10

What potential occupational trends does Figure 24 show?

Figure 24 shows how employment in two cities polarised between 2001 and 2011 in the light of the trends shown in Figure 25. In Stoke-on-Trent, intermediate jobs declined by 8% (12.6% drop in manufacturing jobs) whereas in Peterborough, the decline was *mitigated* by a rise in industrial operatives. In both cities the low wage sectors, especially the care sector, grew far more than the high wage sectors.

The growth of care work: the downside of tertiarisation

Between 1990 and 2012, the care sector's employment had tripled. In 1990, 3.3% worked in the sector and this rose to 6.9% by 2012. It has been predicted that by 2022 the care sector could account for 8.3% of employment. More than 55% of these jobs are in cities, and they are low paid and subject to the effects of recession and austerity. In 2014, 17% of care sector workers were in 'work poverty' (8% nationally for all workers). Many jobs are part-time, involve flexible working and are taken up by women.

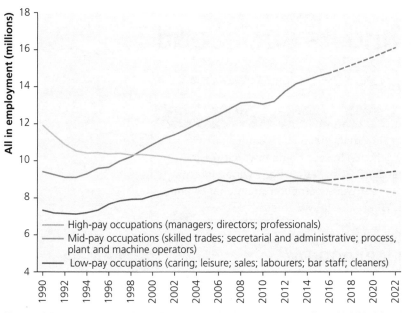

Figure 25 Changes in high-, middle- and low-wage occupations in UK cities 1990–2016 and prediction to 2022

Figure 25 shows that the balance of occupations is changing as the tertiary sector expands.

Fieldwork

Study the distribution of care sector work/care homes in a place both in terms of its scale (perhaps measured by the number of people in a care home), location and the types of property they occupy.

Summary

- Service sector growth has characterised places in advanced economies for over a century.
- Urban centres have been the traditional locations for service sector growth.
- City centres have changed in form and functions to include, offices, retailing and leisure.
- In the late twentieth century, service sector employment spread to other locations within and beyond urban areas.
- Retailing as a city centre service has been challenged by out-of-town and internet shopping.
- Reurbanisation and gentrification are altering the identity of central areas.
- Some central area developments are on former industrial/port areas.

■ The twenty-first-century knowledge economy (quaternary) and its social and economic impacts

Self-study task

Is your home place a university town? How many people are employed in education (universities, colleges and schools) in your home town/city? How many people work within the health sector? Go to Yellow Pages or an internet search site to see if there are computer software, computer maintenance and computer consultancies in the place. Where are they located?

What is the quaternary economy?

The quaternary economy forms the major activity of the 5th Kondratiev wave (Figure 8). It is characterised by the rise of communication and computer and information technologies, and closely allied to the changing nature of communication and transportation systems, which together are producing a set of new townscapes and changed places. Clustering is occurring because productivity and innovation are concentrated in cities. Innovation needs backers, such as city-based financiers and entrepreneurs. Cities have a concentration of creative, digital and professional activities because they have the threshold to support the concentration of a skilled workforce, the existing broadband infrastructure and international trade links.

Intra-industry spillovers are where the proximity of similar firms enables knowledge and ideas to travel among specialist companies, furthering the development of new activities. In 2015, among the smaller players (small- and medium-sized enterprises, or SMEs), 65% of the creative industries and 60% of the digital companies were located in cities.

What follows is a list of terms related to the quarternary economy.

- The knowledge economy is founded upon the ability of people to innovate, which is at the heart of technological change.
- Knowledge Intensive Business Services (KIBS) are still highly localised despite the ability of IT systems to disseminate knowledge to the world. Knowledge tends to be produced in specific places, such as Silicon Valley or Cambridge, and used and improved upon in the same place. 50% of KIBs jobs in city centres are taken by graduates.
- The digital economy employed 6% of the UK workforce (1.3 million people) in 2013. It includes ICT (software development, broadband networks, hardware, software, sales and marketing) and digital content (digital media, publishing, design, music and advertising).

- The creative industries include product design and software development, broadcasting, advertising, libraries and museums.
- Biotechnology and other scientific developments, such as medical research together with legal, accounting and management consultancy, are sometimes included.
- Unicorns are companies that have recently started up and are already worth over US$1billion, e.g. Uber and Airbnb, both of which originated in Silicon Valley. Of the UK unicorns, 13 of the 17 are based in London.

One new job in the digital, knowledge economy leads to five jobs elsewhere in the economy, a feature known as the **multiplier effect**.

One way of measuring innovation and the strength of the knowledge economy is by the number of patents granted (Table 15). At the national level, China, South Korea, Japan, Germany and the USA dominate.

Table 15 Patents granted per 100,000 population 2013

City	Patents granted per 100,000	City	Patents granted per 100,000
Cambridge	65.6	Bolton	0.4
Gloucester	18.5	Sunderland	0.4
Edinburgh	6.2	Wigan	0.6
Sheffield	5.6	—	—
Bristol	5.1	—	—

Where innovation and the knowledge economy are strong, the proportion of the workforce in those places holding high-level qualifications is high. In Cambridge, 66% of the working age population has high-level qualifications, Edinburgh 55%, Oxford 49%, London 48% and Bristol 38%, whereas Burnley, with 19%, Sunderland 22% and Hull 22%, are among the places with the smallest proportions.

Locational factors encouraging cluster growth

Many countries have areas of knowledge economy concentrations, including Silicon Alley, Lower Manhattan, New York (stretching from the Flatiron District to Soho); Cap Digital and Silicon Sentier in the former textile area of Paris; SILICON Wadi in Israel; and MSC Malaysia, formerly the Multimedia Super Corridor, near Kuala Lumpur. Perhaps the best-known among them are Silicon Valley, California, and Silicon Roundabout, in the Old Street area of London. At a smaller scale, the Menai Hub is the promotional name given to the cultural and knowledge-based activities in Bangor, Caernarfon and Llangefni in North Wales.

Silicon Valley, California

Silicon Valley, once called 'the valley of hearts delights' (Figure 26), extends the length of the Santa Clara Valley between San Francisco and San José in California. Until the 1940s it was an area dominated by fruit orchards. Today, it is a set of low-density cities and towns linked by freeways and the Caltrain. The factors (*causality*) that gave rise to the growth of the knowledge-based economy in the valley are as follows:

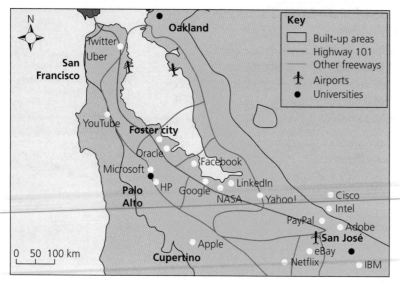

Figure 26 Silicon Valley

1 **Triggers:** the decision by Hewlett-Packard to develop oscillators in their garage in Palo Alto is one starting point. Before that, the area had attracted radio enthusiasts, who began to create an electronics community. The peninsula offered lifestyle benefits to the early innovators; the ocean and the mountains were within easy reach and the Mediterranean climate enabled the development of an outdoor lifestyle that appealed to the young. Until the 1960s, property was cheap and surrounded by orchards, grasslands and forested hills.

2 **The role of Stanford University:** its research professors and students have been a constant source of ideas and innovations that spawned many of the companies that are now found in the region. Other universities in California also played their part in providing researchers and developers, such as San José State, Berkeley and Caltech (*attachment, causality*).

3 **Inspiration of individuals:** Terman, the Dean of Engineering, set up the Stanford Industrial Park in the 1940s, which has attracted over 150 firms. He nudged Hewlett-Packard towards making oscillators. Shockley set up a laboratory in a former fruit-packing plant in Mountain View in 1956 to further develop transistors. Employees of Shockley became dissatisfied and broke away to form Fairchild Semiconductors, which in 1959 produced what would evolve into the silicon chip. One employee set up Intel in Santa Clara, which has become the world's leading chip developer and manufacturer. Other notable individuals are Brin and Page, former students at Stanford, who worked with Filo, the founder of Yahoo, and in 1998 founded Google, now a 13,000-employee campus in Mountain View.

4 **Family trees of companies:** Fairchild became the parent from which offspring hardware companies (Apple, Cisco Systems, Sun Microsystems, Silicon Graphics) emerged. Google, Yahoo, eBay and Netscape piggybacked on the cluster of hardware companies.

5 **Military needs:** during the Second World War and 1950s, military needs resulted in the development of the Ames Research Center at Moffett Field, which

evolved, partially as a result of large government contracts, into a NASA base (*interdependence*).

6 **Young entrepreneurs:** they work for major IT companies where they subsequently develop their own ideas, which they endeavour to take to the market. They require finance from venture capitalists. In the 1960s, the venture capitalist industry developed close to Stanford University in Palo Alto and subsequently elsewhere in the region. These firms clustered close to their clients. Thus finance, just like talent, had agglomerated in the valley (*adaptation, interdependence, risk*).

7 **Talent refuses to leave the area — inertia:** other IT giants arrived because the talent they needed to recruit refused to leave the Bay Area for Redmond, Washington State, Microsoft's HQ, etc. Microsoft recruited a guru named Gray who insisted that the Bay Area Research Centre (BARC) be opened in San Francisco in 1995, which expanded more recently into Mountain View (*attachment, identity*).

8 **Transport provision:** both regionally and internationally, transport provision assisted development. Freeways such as the 101 regularly slow because of the sheer volume of commuters, and the Caltrain line running through the Valley has enabled a myriad commuting patterns between the places. In addition, the presence of major airports, such as San Francisco International, has made it easier to connect to the personalised global economy. There are now more large airports (Oakland International, Mineta San José International), and also small airports such as San Carlos, where the CEO of Oracle has his private jet located a mere five minutes away from the office (*interdependence*).

9 **Ability of firms to recruit talent from around the world:** and especially Asian software engineers (page 17). The range of highly qualified employees (58,000 new jobs were created in 2014 alone) adds to the positive vibes and the growth of success, and increasingly diverse amenities, restaurants and social provision available in the area. This in turn attracts more talent to the agglomeration. Globalisation becomes easier when much of your workforce originates from countries around the world (*globalisation*).

10 **Takeovers:** these are another means by which firms get larger, e.g. Google acquired YouTube, located in San Bruno.

11 **Other organisations moving to the Bay Area to capture talent:** because Silicon Valley and San Francisco Bay are the places to find talent and for new talent to be nurtured, other organisations are moving to the Bay Area. Tesla, the electric car-maker, has its main plant in Fremont, and Airbus announced in 2015 that it is to develop a research facility in the area, rather than in Europe, in order to make use of the expertise. In both of these cases the attraction is the availability of software engineers who can develop improved systems for the modern car or airplane. Biotechnology firms have also used graduate concentration to help them expand in the area. The DOE Joint Genome Institute at Walnut Creek was an early locator, and now firms such as Gilead Sciences have expanded rapidly in Foster City. Major financial organisations, such as Visa in Foster City, have arrived to latch onto the talent pool. Educational innovators are also attracted to the area; in 2016, a French organisation announced that it was setting up a free university in Fremont to train IT workers (*causality, feedback, globalisation*). Table 16 summarises the cost and benefits of Silicon Valley as a *place*.

Table 16 Costs and benefits of the Silicon Valley agglomeration

Costs	Benefits/reactions
Large-scale migration from within the USA and from overseas — leads to:	A cosmopolitan society whose talents can be engaged in a variety of projects
Demand for housing, schools and facilities for young families	Excellent higher education that attracts quality students and researchers
High price of property due to demand exceeding supply, therefore employees are forced to live further away, where prices are lower	Developers building as fast as possible with guaranteed profits; landlords also able to raise rents above inflation
Transport system overloaded — not only in rush hour, due to the 24/7 working pattern	Companies providing own transport that enables work patterns to be more flexible
High levels of pollution	Has led to high levels of hybrid car ownership and the rise of the electric car industry (Tesla)
Water supply issues, especially with summer droughts and extended drought periods (2012–2015)	Environmental awareness is widespread
Older residents feel that the environment and places that they grew up in are being destroyed by progress	The benefits of agglomeration and clustering for transfer of ideas and career progression
Space to build disappearing rapidly, forcing movement onto protected land	Value placed upon spin-offs and new entrepreneurial ventures
Difficulty for public service workers such as teachers to be recruited because of the high price of housing	High levels of highly qualified posts for women
Congestion	The potential to poach quality staff from competitors = knowledge spillover

Silicon Roundabout, Shoreditch, London (Tech City)

Between 2010 and 2016 the most significant locational growth of technical businesses (92% increase in digital firms, 2010–2013) has been in Inner London, where 252,000 work in digital employment. In 2010, Prime Minister David Cameron gave the greatest concentration area its name: Tech City. Also known as Silicon Roundabout, it is an inner urban cluster (*scale*) located within this global city. It is on the fringe of the City CBD and at the eastern end of a high-tech corridor that stretches to the West End. It is a mix of ICT and digital content sectors (Figure 27). The cluster is centred on Old Street roundabout and extends into Hoxton and Haggerston, the City of London, Farringdon and Bethnal Green. The concentration is small compared with other sectors and other wards in London. However, it is an area with a high number of start-ups, especially in the arts and cultural services (*interdependence*).

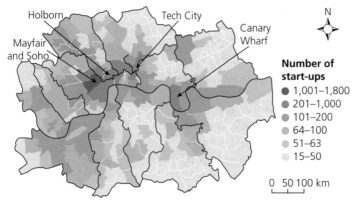

Figure 27 The geography of start-ups in London (2013)

The factors (*causality*) leading to the growth of Tech City are:

1 The amenities of the area, which cater to the new workforce, e.g. café culture and the resultant vibes (*attachment, identity, meaning*)

2 Similar, complementary firms that have clustered in the area; they make use of incubator space in converted Victorian warehouses (*adaptation* and *interdependence*)

3 Branding and messaging that have made both entrepreneurs and financiers aware of the new activities (*causality*)

4 The renting of floor space in the area is far cheaper than in the CBD (*causality*)

5 Proximity to central London and the City, which is the marketplace for the innovations and the source of finance (*interdependence*)

6 Connectivity to the rest of London and the UK

7 Higher broadband speeds than in other parts of central London

One of the effects of Shoreditch's popularity is a doubling in housing rental costs in just two years (2011–2013). Therefore, some entrepreneurs will be forced to look for new, cheaper locations in which to base their start-up.

Transport links will influence the location of newer clusters, such as near King's Cross, where Google, Central St Martins School of Art and Macmillan Group have located on a former goods yard, thus drawing in other new technology ventures (page 85).

Tech firms per square kilometre

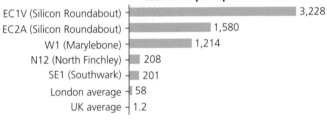

EC1V (Silicon Roundabout)	3,228
EC2A (Silicon Roundabout)	1,580
W1 (Marylebone)	1,214
N12 (North Finchley)	208
SE1 (Southwark)	201
London average	58
UK average	1.2

Figure 28 The main areas for start-ups in London 2008–2011

Figure 28 illustrates where clusters grow, often in areas that are already the focus of that particular activity. Activity in finance, culture and the arts is very concentrated, whereas professional services and ICT are more dispersed. Figure 28 measures the density of tech firms in London in 2015.

Education and its impact on cities

If you live in a university town you are probably very aware of the impact of the student population (including the employees of education establishments) on both the housing market and the provision of services.

In 2010/11, Birmingham had 57,115 full-time students in its three universities. Likewise, Manchester had over 50,000 in its three universities. Coventry had 35,265 students in its university and FE college, whereas there were 15,572 in York. While many students live in halls of residence, some of which are privately rented, a large proportion are housed in the private rented sector. We have already seen how students play a key part in the gentrification of city centres in their new halls of residence (page 51).

Impacts of quaternary industry clusters on people and places

Business and science parks have developed around many towns and cities. Cambridge developed the first science park in 1973. Thirteen such sites now function in up to a 10-mile radius around the city. The university and highly skilled graduates combined with the conserved historic core have attracted KIBS jobs to the city and pushed up living costs. Even within the city, a new knowledge industry space is being developed around the railway station, which has already attracted Microsoft and will house Cambridge Assessment, the giant international examination board. Some cities have over-supplied these locations, e.g. Newcastle-upon-Tyne, often using their EZ status (pages 43–44), and several sites in the city remain under-occupied.

The impact of quaternary activity on people, localities and places is summarised in Figures 29 and 30. **Digital exclusion** refers to a lack of skills associated with computers together with poor access to broadband. Rural areas (e.g. Northumberland, Anglesey) are most likely to exclude people due to the lack of access to broadband, because there is not the threshold population to support the investment in cabling in these regions. In Pembrokeshire, 22.8% of adults have never been online. The reasons for low use of digital technologies are varied and include a more elderly population, out-migration of young adults to universities, no training for the older generation and a lack of jobs in the area.

Knowledge check 11

Use Figure 30 to describe and offer explanations for digital company growth. Is the data displayed in the best format?

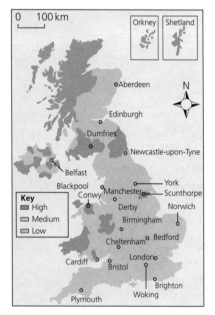

Figure 29 Likelihood of digital exclusion in the UK

Bournemouth	212%
Liverpool	119%
Inner London	92%
Brighton & Hove	91%
South Wales	87%
Belfast	73%
Greater Manchester	70%
Bristol & Bath	65%
Hull	57%
Birmingham	51%
Cambridge	46%
Edinburgh	33%
Oxford	24%
North East	24%
Norwich	21%
Sheffield	17%
UK average	53%

Figure 30 Digital company growth 2010–2013

Urban areas (e.g. Woking, Guildford, Southampton, Aberdeen, Warwick) are less excluded from broadband, resulting in low levels of exclusion overall. However, there are some urban areas, such as North Lincolnshire around Scunthorpe and Rhondda Cynon Taf, where having access to broadband, low educational attainment and relative poverty can lead to social exclusion (*inequality*).

South Wales, and especially Cardiff, has seen a growing number employed in the tech sector (28,000 in 2015). Proximity to the Welsh government in Cardiff Bay and government support via the Business Wales Digital Development Fund have helped. That staff and space are cheaper than elsewhere in the UK has aided the establishment of the Innovation Centre for Enterprise (ICE) in Caerphilly, one of the most deprived towns in Wales (*mitigation*).

Summary

- Quaternary activities are of increasing importance in both urban and rural places.
- The factors determining the location of quaternary activity include some that were important for secondary industry, such as clustering, but also factors that are related to the importance of new technologies and entrepreneurship in the twenty-first century.
- Educational hubs and research centres are important attractions for digital and biotech companies.
- Quaternary, knowledge-based activities are being driven by large multinational companies and at the same time, small independent companies/individuals that have spun off from the global companies.
- Some people are excluded from these new activities and are unable to benefit from the use of new technologies.

The rebranding process and players in rural places

The decline in primary employment in rural areas

You should distinguish between **rurality**, the degree to which an area of the natural, non-urban world depends on agriculture/food/forestry, and **peripherality**, the distance either in time or space from the opportunities provided by urban areas. A total of 80% of employment in rural areas in England is in jobs other than agriculture/fishing (7%) and tourism (12%).

Since 2004, rural areas have been defined as areas in which no settlement is greater than 10,000 people. Rural areas are divided into sparse (low density of dwellings) and less sparse (higher density of dwellings, see Figure 31). Those areas classified as sparse are not necessarily what a geographer would class as remote rural, although some are remote.

A different classification (Figure 32) recognises that urban influence and access extends to large areas around cities either as 'suburbs' or 'hinterland', all of which extend well into the countryside. Very little rural land is left.

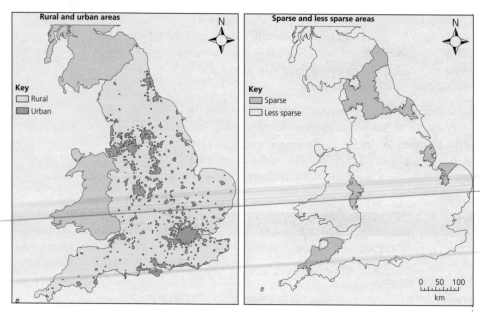

Figure 31 Rural/urban classifications in England

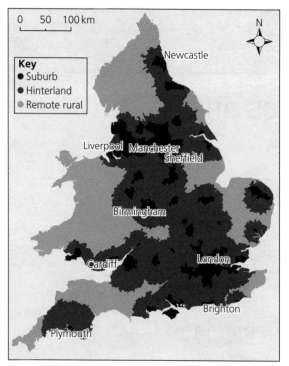

Figure 32 Suburbs, hinterland and more remote rural areas (2015)

Figure 33 illustrates how much employment in rural areas altered between 2008 and 2012 (*difference*). In 2011, only 1% of the rural population worked in primary employment.

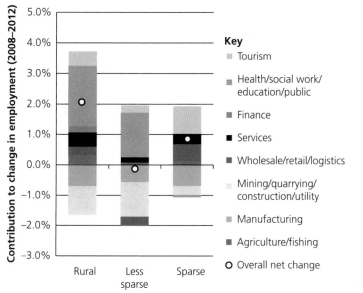

Figure 33 Employment change in rural areas of England (2008–2012)

Rural areas, which comprise 7.4% of the land area of England and Wales, are further classified as:

a 'minor' built-up areas, those with a population of under 10,000

b town and fringe

c village

d hamlet and isolated dwellings.

Also, all categories (b) to (d) are subdivided further by adding 'sparse' areas characterised by low population densities, Table 17. In 2011, 18.5% of the population of England and Wales lived in rural areas and 33% in the rural hinterlands, the areas from which people commute to a city, around cities. Over 20% of these people work in a city. In Wales, 32.8% live in rural areas.

Table 17 The percentage of residents aged between 16 and 74 in rural settlements (after 2011 census)

Type of rural area	Population 2011 (million)	% population England and Wales	% growth 2001–2011
Town and fringe	4.8	8.6	6.1
Town and fringe in sparse areas	0.3	0.5	4.3
Village	3.2	5.8	5.3
Village in sparse areas	0.3	0.5	3.7
Hamlets and isolated dwellings	1.7	3.5	5.3
Hamlets in a sparse setting	0.25	0.4	2.8

The rural idyll

Rural areas have been idyll-ised in many people's representations. People tend to focus on rural natural landscapes that they wish to conserve, due to inherent beauty/ruggedness or because they live there. Rural areas are where our food is produced, for the big supermarkets and organic, local and sustainable small-scale retailers. Rural living has a 'gloss' that tends to hide socially excluded groups, such as travellers. Figure 34 schematises the rural idyll and how it is perceived (*identity*).

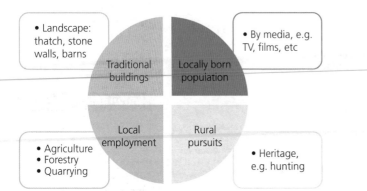

- Landscape: thatch, stone walls, barns

Traditional buildings

Locally born population

- By media, e.g. TV, films, etc

Local employment

Rural pursuits

- Agriculture
- Forestry
- Quarrying

- Heritage, e.g. hunting

Figure 34 The rural idyll and how it is perceived

Self-study task

Study Figure 35, which shows the village of Claverley in Shropshire. How far does the view seen in the figure support the concept of the rural idyll? What might the population composition be? What challenges, risks and issues might confront the population?

Figure 35 Claverley, Shropshire

Why has the primary workforce declined?

1 **Technological developments replace human labour:** in Thomas Hardy's nineteenth-century Wessex the reaper and binder took away jobs; last century, increasingly sophisticated combine harvesters, picking technology and machinery for raising root crops replaced human labour. There has also been a rise in agriunits, which cultivate crops (such as tomatoes) under controlled conditions (such as using CO_2 from the ICI Teesside chemical industry) (*adaptation, causality, mitigation*).

2 **Rising scale of farms:** farms have grown and small family farms have merged. Supermarkets demand economies of scale, which has been especially evident in dairy farming (*scale*).

3 **Rise in factory farming:** not just of livestock and birds, but also salad vegetables picked, priced and packed in industrial units (*adaptation*).

4 **Year-round crops:** a demand for the supply of certain crops both in and out of season has increased supply from foreign, usually cheaper, suppliers, e.g. Kenyan runner beans and Spanish tomatoes (*adaptation*).

> **Exam tip**
>
> Primary economic activity includes forestry, fishing and quarrying. Be sure to be ready with examples of the reasons for the loss of jobs in these industries.

Diversification in the countryside through reimaging and regenerating rural places

The media presents a nostalgic version of the countryside. The film and play *War Horse* and TV programmes such as *Emmerdale, Downton Abbey, The Vicar of Dibley, Doc Martin, Hidden Villages* and *Escape to the Country* all reinforce perceptions of rural areas (*identity*). Large country houses are used to promote sales of cars and as the site of promotional and exhibition events, e.g. the Festival of Speed and the Revival Festival attract 200,000 visitors over four days and 148,000 over three days respectively to the Goodwood estate each year. Former rural activities sites are used to provide further recreation:

- The Amberley Museum & Heritage Centre: an industrial heritage centre, in a former chalk quarry (*adaptation*)
- St Fagans National History Museum: on the site of a castle donated for the purpose (*identity*)
- Gressenhall Farm & Workhouse: formerly a 'house of industry for the poor' and workhouse, converted in rural Norfolk (*adaptation, difference*)
- Combe Martin: the village uses customs associated with its historical mythology to attract visitors, such as the weekend event 'Hunting the Earl of Rune'. The event is centuries old, but local groups and businesses now utilise it to reimage and bring income to the village (*adaptation, attachment, resilience*).
- Primary activities employ 40,000 people or 2.8% of the labour force in Wales.

Managing rural change

Since the 1980s, the rural population has increased as a result of **counter-urbanisation**, the movement of jobs and people out from cities to smaller towns and rural areas. This movement began with the relocation of manufacturing to the New Towns, outside of major cities, but the areas are now dominated by tertiary and quarternary jobs.

People also migrated to gain the perceived advantages of rural life, while retaining the attributes of urban living, such as urban media, telecommunications and transport availability. Nevertheless, rural areas are dominated by the over-55s and the young still migrate to the cities to study and/or work. 25% of the 630,000 people living in Welsh rural areas are over 65 years old.

Reimaging Corwen project

Corwen (population 2,325), Denbighshire, is an example of a set of regeneration and arts-based projects (*adaptation* and *mitigation*) having a positive effect on the region. A key regeneration strategy is to extend the Llangollen Heritage Railway (*heritage*) from Carog into Corwen, the first phase of which opened in 2014, in order to bring in more tourists (*recreation*). With funding from the Arts Council of Wales' Ideas:People:Places Fund (*external agency*), a disused field is to be converted into a community garden (*local groups*). There is also continuing funding for an artist-in-residence and a range of visiting artists to work with the community (*events management*). Corwen is part of the 'Shape My Town' project, during which the Design Commission for Wales (*external agency*) is providing a guide 'for how to investigate the quality of their place, town, village or neighbourhood and identify what makes a place unique and to plan for the future by investing time and money in improving it'.

Shape My Town

The Design Commission for Wales, and architects in practice and in universities developed this project in order to encourage the involvement of people in the development of the place in which they live. Ruthin is one village that has participated; with only 5,461 population, it retains a rural centre character.

Local initiative reimaging: Cartmel

Cartmel (Figure 36) is a village of 1,500 people outside of the Lake District National Park, which has reinvented itself as a place with a distinct identity. At the heart of the village is the 12th-century Priory Church and the village square with its 16th–18th-century buildings. There is a small traditional steeplechase racecourse just outside of the village. The village website states that 'Cartmel is not trapped in time. The village offers today's visitors many modern surprises in the form of quality attractions, shops, eateries and places to stay.' Reimaging in Cartmel can be traced back to 1993 (*time, risk*), when the new owners of the village shop took the initiative to close the post office and move into the marketing of souvenirs, including the Cartmel sticky toffee pudding. They had the foresight to patent the name, which provides further income and has aided the improvement of the village store.

> **Exam tip**
>
> All of the terms shown in italic refer to elements of diversification of place. You should be able to quote each of them in relation to your place.

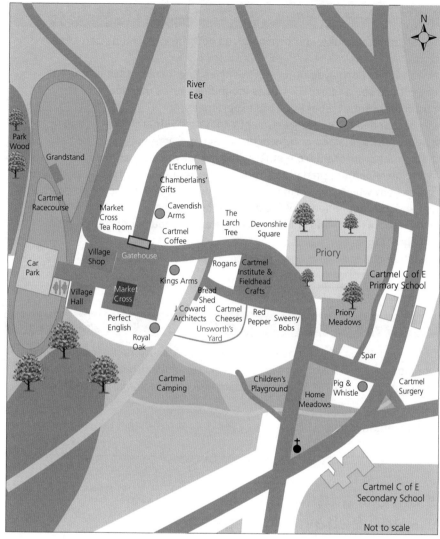

Figure 36 Cartmel: villagers' representation

Self-study task

Using a rural area/place near you for research purposes, does the employment in the area look similar to that shown in Figure 36?

In 2002 (*time*), Simon Rogan, who had trained as a chef in various hotels in Hampshire, established L'Enclume in the old forge. The restaurant soon gained two Michelin stars and such is its reputation that he has developed a bistro and a pub in the village. Other food providers have located in the village to benefit from the growing gastronomic cluster, such as a cheese shop and a quality wine shop (*threshold*). Indirect publicity via Chris Evans on Radio 2 has also resulted in more people discovering Cartmel and, in turn, more visitors travelling there (*media*). Even the racecourse is now the venue for stadium-style concerts in the summer months. In 2014, the village produced the Cartmel Township Initiative (note that both town and village are used in the publicity): www.cartmelvillage.com

Use the Cartmel website mentioned above to make your own notes on how the village illustrates the following key concepts.

- *Representation:* how Cartmel was and is portrayed by formal agencies (the local council or tourist board) and people. What these groups see and experience as inhabitants or as managers.
- *Identity:* how change is seen from different perspectives and experiences.
- *Adaptation:* how the village has responded to reduce its current and future vulnerability to change.
- *Attachment:* the linkages between individuals and groups to the village of Cartmel.
- *Difference:* the ways in which Cartmel is different from other villages that you have studied.
- *Globalisation:* the impact of world development on nations, regions, settlements and localities. Where do visitors come from? The process by which the world is becoming increasingly interconnected as a result of increased integration and interdependence of the global economy.
- *Sustainability:* local planning that meets the needs of the present village without compromising the ability of future communities to meet their own needs.
- *Resilience:* the ability of a population and the historic buildings to adapt to changes that may have a negative impact.

Fieldwork

Contrast two rural settlements, their services, population size and structure, employment, housing and community spirit. The theme is the changing nature of place.

You could demonstrate a range of quantitative and qualitative skills depending on the focus of the study, including numerical measurements (cartographic and graphical skills) and non-numerical techniques (interviews, images, mental maps and texts).

The consequences of rebranding on perceptions, actions and behaviour of people

Rebranding can have a range of outcomes for and effects on people. Some people are attached to the memories of a past 'golden age', a process called **habituation** or **NIMBYism** (Not In My Back Yard), with the consequence that they wish the village to remain as it once was (especially at the time when they moved to the village from urban areas, seeking the rural idyll). Very often, rebranding of a village seeks to play up past images.

Rebranding can also harness perceptions of a community and community spirit by encouraging volunteering in place of local government services.

Rebranding Blaenau Ffestiniog

Blaenau Ffestiniog, Wales was founded as a town based on primary industry (the quarrying of slate). Its peak population was 11,274 in 1881, but the decline of quarrying has led to a decline in population, just 4,900 in 2011. In the later twentieth century, the townspeople had attempted to rebrand the town as a tourist centre (Ffestiniog Railway, Llechwedd Slate Caverns). But they wanted something more, especially a foothold in the growing adventure tourism industry. Regeneration of the town has been a result of both private and public partnership:

- Blaenau Ymlaen was set up in 2006 as a local partnership between the community and the researchers developing the project. It was difficult to gain funding due to the scars of large-scale quarrying (*rebranding*).
- Local authority Gwynedd County Council, together with the Welsh Government and European Union funding, worked to improve public areas such as the town centre (*external funding*).
- The town was boosted by receiving awards from the Royal Town Planning Institute, the Institute of Civil Engineers Wales, and becoming the Towns Alive Environment and Culture winner in 2013 (*actions of people*).
- Antur Stiniog 2007 was a locally developed community initiative that established mountain bike trails in the region. Today, Antur employs 19 people, who administer the trails together with an outdoor equipment shop in the town centre. It also runs a fell-running competition, walking, kayaking, caving, nature and history trails (*changing businesses, tourism*).
- The 2015 Velorail was established, using sustainable bike technology along a disused rail line (*recreation*).
- Zip World Titan was built in the old quarries, to the point that their spatial extent is greater than anywhere else in Europe (*recreation, tourism*).
- Bounce Below (giant trampolines and slides) was assembled in a former slate mine (*recreation, tourism*).
- The project Y Dref Werdd (Renew Wales) addresses sustainability by working to reduce social problems among the population, improving the health of the population and creating a community of stakeholders (*behaviour of people*) who are passionate about the environment and who contribute to community development. The project has developed new allotments and is introducing smart energy to the village (*local community*).

The Great British High Street competition

The Great British High Street competition (page 84) has also awarded villages for their efforts to reimage themselves. In 2015, West Kilbride in Ayrshire, Scotland won for transforming itself into a craft village, supporting local artists and turning around the village perception with creativity and enthusiasm (*local community*).

Knowledge check 14

In 2014, 250,000 visitors came to Blaenau Ffestiniog. However, the older generation are sceptical about success — why?

Exam tip

Do not forget that forest economies employ 40,000 people in the UK. Can you summarise the changes to a forest area near you?

Summary

- Not all rural areas are peripheral areas.
- Population is growing in most rural areas due to counter-urbanisation, return migration to rural areas.
- Movement to rural areas is often on the basis of the perceptions of rural places, the rural idyll.
- Employment in primary occupations in rural areas is declining.
- Employment in rural areas is diversifying.
- Rural places are reimaging themselves either with governmental assistance or through private initiatives.

■ Rural management and the challenges of continuity and change

What are the processes of change that are affecting rural areas?

Demographic

Rural population is changing both in its demographic characteristics and location. People in rural areas had a mean age of 45 in 2011 compared with 42 in 2001, as the 'baby boomers' retire to the country. Figure 37 compares the age profile in 2001 and 2011. One-person (age 65+) households formed 14% of rural households and other single person households (13%) in 2011. Many are returnees to their place of birth, which has been estimated to be as high as 18% of all movement into rural areas in parts of Wales. Rural populations are generally healthier, despite the age of the population.

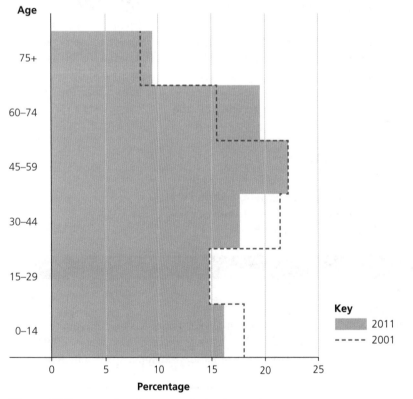

Figure 37 The age of resident population in rural areas 2001 and 2011

Counter-urbanisation

Migration of higher and middle-income groups from urban areas seeking affordable property has swelled rural numbers. Figure 38 gives data on occupations of rural residents in 2011 and it is notable that approximately one-third of those employed are in high-status, high-salaried jobs.

All too often counter-urbanisation is portrayed as individuals escaping the polluted, harried city for a more down-to-earth way of life in the country. Some of what is often called counter-urbanisation is actually rural-to-rural migration, which studies in Wales and Scotland have shown to number one-quarter of migrants. Many of these migrants have higher incomes than those leaving urban areas.

These are the traditional counter-urbanising people, able to commute to urban areas for work and shopping, and subsequently retire in the village or hamlet. This is a fast-growing characteristic of the rural areas fringing cities and towns. Areas fringing cities in southern England up to 130–180 km from London are under pressure to expand. Here, rural settlements are in high-quality countryside, within easy reach of rail and motorways, and have inhabitants whose work patterns and lifestyles are urban. Affluent rural areas (the home of 'Motorway Man') surround the growing urban areas of the south. These are the classic sites for counter-urbanisation and give rise to pressures on land and housing for the diminishing number of primary industry employees and young people. In contrast, in the north of England and in parts of Wales, motorways and rural lifestyle have attracted people into the countryside from towns and cities suffering from deindustrialisation and multiple deprivation. Counter-urbanisation is from deprived towns such as Burnley, Preston and Bradford to affluent rural areas such as Ribble Valley, Wyre and Craven. This has the following effects on the area:

- **Lower income local buyers:** local buyers can be priced out and the social mix of places altered as a result.

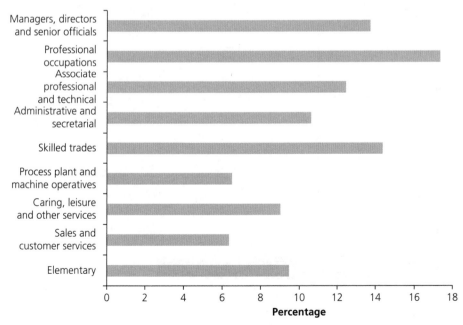

Figure 38 Occupations of rural residents aged 16–74 in England and Wales (2011)

- **Second-home ownership:** second-home owners take properties out of the local market, which affects all areas, especially more sparsely peopled districts. In Cornwall, the takeovers have been so great that communities are looking at ways of alleviating the effects. In Scotland, ultra-high net worth individuals, often global investors, invest in Scottish rural estates and encourage a change in the nature of the rural economy towards leisure pursuits.
- **Owner occupation:** levels of home ownership are higher in rural areas (74%) compared with urban areas (61%). This is partly a result of counter-urbanisation.
- **Low incomes in the primary and care sectors:** low incomes lead to resource deprivation, an inability to obtain affordable housing and opportunity deprivation (the difficulties involved in accessing services such as health and recreation). Increasing skill requirements in all forms of primary activity leads to a greater chance of unemployment among those who lack qualifications. Rural people may experience in-work poverty.
- **Mobility deprivation:** for example, refusing driving licences for the elderly on the grounds of poor health, rising transport costs, availability of public transport as rural bus subsidies are cut, all of which leads to the inaccessibility of jobs and services.
- **Digital exclusion:** Figure 29 on page 64 identifies the areas in which digital exclusion is prevalent. You should be able to explain this in terms of peripherality, population densities and distance.
- **Poverty:** for some, poverty is one outcome. People are unable to share in the lifestyle of the majority in a small settlement because they lack the resources to do so.

Rural populations can be overly disadvantaged. Although the characteristics of deprivation are similar to those in urban areas, many have a disproportionate effect, which leads to a self-sustaining spiral of rural deprivation. Peripherality and isolation only make the effects of deprivation worse. Figure 39 summarises the forces that lead to reimaged rural places.

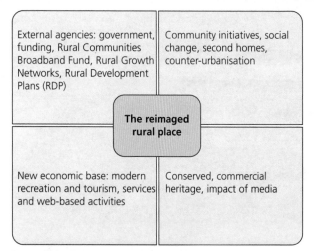

Figure 39 The reimaged rural place

Fieldwork

Study rural deprivation in a county. Begin with secondary source data and then examine the characteristics of the places where rural deprivation is statistically higher or lower. How are these places represented?

Managing rural change and inequality in diverse communities

People tend to visualise places in their minds. The variety of people living in rural areas will inevitably result in different perceptions and understanding of the nature of that village or locality. In the mid-twentieth century, Ceredigion and Montgomeryshire had a declining population. This coloured the perceptions of these places as being static and failing to move with the times. On the other hand, some saw this as an opportunity to acquire cheaper second homes. This in turn raised opposition from the local population and resulted in the attempted burning of some second homes. Infrastructure, access to schools and health facilities were poor, but these issues did not concern the second-home owners because they could return to the cities (*identity*).

Second-home ownership

Over 165,000 people own holiday homes in England and Wales. The greatest number of second homes is in Cornwall (23,000), whereas Gwynedd (7,784) has more per head of resident population. Other concentrations include North Norfolk (4,842), South Hams, Devon (3,738), South Lakeland, Cumbria (4,684) and the Isles of Scilly (99 holiday home owners in a population of 2,203). This tends to result in the pushing up of house prices and long-term rentals in the most popular tourist regions, all out of reach of the local workers on low wages. In 2016, St Ives, Cornwall held a referendum to ascertain whether the area, in which 1 in 5 houses in the town and district were already second homes, should permit more second homes (subsequently, reports clarified that the referendum was related to the introduction of new properties rather than all types of properties).

> **Fieldwork**
>
> If you live in an area with many second homes, investigate where the owners come from, or what the local community/individuals think of the rise of second homes and their impact on local services.

The 'Lakes by yoo' development

> 'The Lakes by yoo is a 650-acre private development, set in glorious parkland, comprising of lakes and woodland and meadows, in the heart of The Cotswolds. The estate features idyllic properties with interiors designed by Kate Moss, Elle McPherson, Jade Jagger, Kelly Hoppen and Phillipe Starck. Interested? View for more details at www.thelakesbyyoo.com.'

The 'Lakes by yoo' development is a 650-acre (263ha) private estate in the Cotswolds. In this case, property experts Humberts are selling second homes on the basis of privacy and the rural idyll, and they use 'celebrity' names as a promotional tool (*identity, representation*).

Transport, health and service provision

The lack of transport in rural areas is a cause of growing inequality. People travel further than urban dwellers and mainly by car (59%), but 11% do not have access to a

Knowledge check 15

What do the Figures 37–39 tell you about the nature of the issues faced by rural settlements and rural communities in England and Wales?

Exam tip

Be wary of your data sources and whether they may be biased. The figures given in the text for second-home ownership in districts do not mention whether the owners are joint rather than individual owners of the properties. Also, the St Ives reporting initially implied that it was to stop even existing second homes being subject to the ban when they were sold, which was later shown to be false.

car (compared with 28% in urban areas). This reflects the relative wealth of the new rural population and the relative poverty of the long-term residents. Surveys have shown that one-third of rural residents find public transport inadequate because of irregular service and fitting in with working hours, school and service provision times (*isolation*).

As the proportion of elderly residents rises, supporting the health needs of the people living in rural areas is an increasing challenge. The percentage of people with disability or health problems that limit activity is higher in rural than in urban areas. This is particularly so in the more remote areas (*peripherality*).

Service provision can be under threat in some communities. With few shops left in villages, the closure of a post office is seen as a threat. Where possible, the service is moved in to share with another use but there has to be an alternative site. Businesses no longer wish to be associated with a post office (*mitigation, adaptation*). Some chains have opened village stores, but their profits leave the village and the effect on local spending is small. Banks have also been closing — 243 in rural areas in 2014 as a result of the success of online banking. However, poor broadband speeds in more remote areas have had an impact on a community where access to broadband is limited (*isolation*).

On the other hand, rural-to-rural migrants remain in rural occupations, together with branching out into food and accommodation businesses, which can employ others. Those coming from the cities and towns are more likely to set up arts and crafts and IT-related businesses, which rarely employ extra staff. Younger migrants into the country earn more and are in higher professional occupations. The reasons for moving to or between rural areas are shown in Table 18.

Table 18 Motivations for moving to rural areas

Motivation	Counter-urban migrants	Rural-to-rural migrants
Employment	11%	22%
Housing	3%	10%
Nearer parents/adult children	10%	10%
Retirement (planning for or actual)	33%	28%
Quality of life	26%	15%
Other	17%	14%

Stockdale, Aileen (2015) 'Contemporary and 'Messy' Rural In-migration Processes: Comparing Counter-urban and Lateral Rural Migration' in *Population, Place and Space* (John Wiley & Sons).

Ongoing challenges in rural places with regeneration/rebranding

Some of the greatest challenges face rural settlements that are too small to be the subject of a major regeneration scheme. The challenges of a small population threshold are being addressed by minor changes that may impact on the community, for example:

■ In the UK, there are over 350 community-run shop and/or post offices, some staffed by volunteers. An estimated 300–500 village shops close every year. Since 2010, an average of 22 shops have opened under community ownership each year.

Pwllglas Community Shop, near Ruthin, Barford Village Shop in Warwickshire and St Tudy Community Shop and Post Office in Cornwall are examples of this trend.

- Forncett St Peter, Norfolk have used an old telephone box as a site in which to house a defibrillator, which caters for health emergencies in the remote village.
- In North Stoke, a village in West Sussex, a local 'library' and visitor guide point has been placed in a disused red telephone box.

Self-study task

Figure 39 schematises the four components of reimaging rural places. Using a village or hamlet that you know, attempt to place any rebranding and regeneration initiatives in one of the boxes. Have the efforts succeeded — if so, why?

Fieldwork

Here are three opportunities for study:
1 Changing provision of services in contrasting villages.
2 The impact of a community shop on a small settlement.
3 Social and economic characteristics of suburbanised villages.

New challenges of managing change associated with counter-urbanisation and second-home ownership

Community Land Trusts

Community Land Trusts (CLT) are one strategy being used to counteract the pressure of counter-urbanisation and second homes. CLTs were first used in the USA during the Civil Rights Movement of the 1960s, and in areas of urban housing shortage. The principle was brought to the UK and the National CLT Charity was launched in 2014 as a response to the early success of CLTs. CLTs are themselves a response to the loss of services (shops, post offices, doctors' surgeries) and high house prices as counter-urbanisation changes the settlement (*adaptation, mitigation, risk, sustainability*). For more details on CLTs, go to www.communitylandtrusts.org.uk.

Angmering CLT in West Sussex has been in existence since 2013 and is sponsored by the Parish Council. It is currently forming itself into a Community Benefit Society. The aim is to focus on providing affordable housing within the parish because the under-30s can no longer afford to buy property in the village. Eight houses on a housing development of several hundred homes are being bought by the Trust to rent to local people. In addition, the CLT aims to re-establish lost community facilities, such as local shops.

St David's Peninsula CLT in Pembrokeshire hopes to build 118 homes on a site of 3.6ha in the city of St David's. It is intended to include a swimming pool and café in the development. The work has attracted more community involvement than has occurred previously.

'The ultimate vision is to maintain the historic communities of the St David's peninsula [*heritage*], their schools, institutions and services, by enabling young local families to live and thrive in the area to which they belong.'

CLT Minutes 2015

Exam tip

If you use secondary sources, especially in your fieldwork, remember to say so.

CLTs have to be constituted so that they may buy, sell and rent property and be eligible to obtain loans. Re-sale of owned properties is restricted to 30% of the market value. Local inhabitants have the first right to buy or rent.

Policies to restrict second homes

- Removing council tax subsidy of 10%.
- Placing quota on second-home building (used in Canton of Valais, Switzerland).
- Designating properties that can be used for holiday lets and second homes rather than permitting all to be available for these purposes.
- Capital gains tax concessions on the sale of these properties could be withdrawn.

Fieldwork

Conduct a study of the effect of a rural CLT to see how it is altering the place or places in which it is located.

Foreign Direct Investment

Foreign Direct Investment is also being used to regenerate some rural areas in which there has been a loss of primary activity. Investors from the USA, in partnership with a UK company, are proposing to transform a former open-cast mining site near Chesterfield, Derbyshire into a health, sport and education facility, which should create 1,000 new jobs.

Summary

- The processes of change in rural areas include the demographic, counter-urbanisation and housing market changes.
- An outcome of change is rural deprivation and poverty, which is very dispersed and may not be revealed by local area statistics.
- Second homes and holiday homes put pressure on the housing market.
- Efforts are being made at local governmental and community levels to address the problems of deprivation, the provision of services, housing and isolation in rural areas.

The rebranding process and players in urban places

Towns and cities compete as places to attract investment. In this urge to compete, those in power project images of a place that they know will attract the investment that they want. Canary Wharf has been successful not only because it benefited from Urban Development Corporation financial support from the government, but because the place reflects the images of the finance industry (high-rise buildings, well-dressed and well-qualified people commuting to work in a district that contains restaurants, bars, shops, hotels and apartments to cater for the high-earners). This is in marked contrast to the working-class and immigrant population — employed in the docks and living in terraced housing with a lack of infrastructure — that had characterised the place before 1980. The location is the same but the place has changed; the Isle of Dogs has been rebranded as Canary Wharf.

Reimaging and rebranding urban places

Reimaging and rebranding is sometimes called **boosterism**. The way a place is 'boosted' can change over time; Chicago was once called 'Gem of the Prairies' before it received negative publicity as 'Hogopolis' and 'Cornopolis', whereas today, 'the Windy City' is a more benign tagline. Cities now promote both business opportunities and lifestyle opportunities, as shown in Table 19.

Table 19 Types of city promotion

Business promotion	Lifestyle promotion
Centrality	'Most liveable city'
Accessibility	Cultural centrality
Communication costs	Centre of action — clubs, bars, theatres, sport
Landscapes of modernity — clean, flagship buildings	Leisure time and refined leisure facilities
Specialist and quality skills — HE institutions	Access to countryside
Global links — airports, international train stations	—

Self-study task

Look at your local town or city's publicity online or in a brochure, and link what you discover to the typology in Table 19.

Culture-led regeneration

Culture-led regeneration was initially inspired by the success of the Guggenheim Museum in Bilbao, Spain. It is one method of promoting economic regeneration. European City of Culture designation commenced in 1985 and, so far, two UK cities have been designated — Glasgow in 1990, with its strapline 'Glasgow's miles better', and Liverpool in 2008. In 2009, a UK City of Culture distinction was established, Londonderry taking the mantle in 2013 while Hull is the next city in the four-yearly cycle (2017).

Fieldwork

What have been the effects of these titles on the built environment and lives of people in the cities that were selected?

Gateshead Quayside in Newcastle-upon-Tyne, including the Millennium Bridge, the Baltic Centre of Contemporary Art (formerly the Baltic Flour Mill) and the Sage Gateshead concert venue, is another prime example of regeneration, at a cost of £142m. Some jobs elsewhere in Newcastle could possibly be attributed to this development, but it seems to have had little effect on job creation in the immediate area. Rather, it had other impacts in terms of the actual and perceived image of the city (*identity*).

In Bradford, the establishment of the Museum of Photography, Film and Television in 1983 and its achieving the first UNESCO City of Film status in 2009 have been pivotal in allowing regeneration to take place. In addition, the Moorside Mills (1875) that once wove worsted and lay derelict since 1970 were converted into an Industrial Museum, opened in 1975.

The Turner Contemporary Gallery, which opened in 2011, has brought an extra £41m spending to Margate in five years as the result of approximately 200,000 extra visitors to the town who are visiting the gallery. It has resulted in a boutique hotel opening in 2013 in a converted old seafront hotel, and many more restaurants and arts-related retailing.

Multi-functional redevelopments that contain theatres as well as retailing, cinemas and even local government facilities have been favoured, but these tend to drain people away from the traditional high street. Theatre restoration can also be part of cultural regeneration. Farmers' markets and Christmas markets are other forms of cultural regeneration designed to return shoppers to town centres. Christmas markets are frequently identified with the German model in an attempt to provide an image that is associated with affluence and possibly mitigate the declining status of a CBD's retail district.

Sports stadia

Stadia are frequently used as the catalyst for regeneration, although the trigger is often the result of the global pressure of hosting major sporting events, as the list below demonstrates:

- Don Valley Stadium, Sheffield (1991): World Student Games
- Principality Stadium (originally Millennium Stadium), Cardiff (1999): Rugby World Cup, City Centre site
- City of Manchester Stadium (now Etihad Stadium): built to host the Commonwealth Games (2002), 1.6 km from the city centre on a brownfield site and part of East Manchester Sportcity
- Olympic Stadium and Park (2012), East London

The costs and benefits of stadia developments are summarised in Table 20.

Table 20 Costs and benefits of major stadia developments

Benefits	Costs/disbenefits
Can underpin regeneration goals	Congestion
Generate jobs	Accessibility for large numbers (e.g. Wembley)
Increased commercial activity	Noise and light pollution
Multiplier effect of the benefits above	Quality of life of residents (i.e. NIMBYism)
Bring tax income to local council and country	Property values may decline
Create landmark site that identifies the place/city	High maintenance costs
Increased tourism (e.g. stadium tours, visiting fans, hotels)	Shortfalls in income from occasional use
Increased community provision	Conversion costs (e.g. Olympic Park)
Generate civic pride	Policing on match days
Image improvement	Vandalism, graffiti, litter
Raise sponsors' profile (e.g. Amex, Brighton; Etihad, Manchester)	
Revive property prices (e.g. Cardiff)	
Catalyst for property renovation (e.g. Cardiff)	

Other stadia have been relocated to enable the former site to be used for other activities. The Amex Stadium, Brighton enabled the former Goldstone Ground to be sold for housing. Other such changes have been completed in Reading, Swansea, Southampton and Highbury. Stadia are invariably multi-purpose and are used as venues for pop/rock concerts, community activities and conferences, which make use of the building's administrative space.

Fieldwork

If you live in a town where there has been a stadium relocation it should be possible to examine the effect of relocation on the nature of its former and new locations.

Reimaging and regenerating economies

Rebranding requires places to shed their old image and to metamorphose into new, reimaged places that use the past as a part of the new brand image (*adaptation, identity, representation*).

Local authority government rebranding

In 2013 there were 137 **Business Improvement Districts (BIDs)** in urban areas. Newcastle NE1 is one such scheme, and started in 2009. The Newcastle initiatives target the needs of city centre retail businesses after 5 p.m., aiming to:

- extend shop opening hours with free parking.
- build on the 4.3 million extra visitors to the Eldon Square shopping centre that followed
- improve access to the Central Station, which was achieved as a result of BID obtaining £5m from the ERDF, Network Rail and the City
- use vacant shops as spaces for youth training, employment support, entertainment and socialising (Space 2).

BIDS in smaller settlements are less successful because retailers and services are expected to contribute to the scheme. In Skipton, some services such as hairdressers resent contributing to a scheme designed to attract tourists. It pays to be wary of job creation figures in regeneration projects because most overestimate job creation by up to 40%.

Fieldwork

Examine the impact of a BIDS scheme in a place that you know. How does it affect the lives of the people in the place?

Tramshed, in Grangetown, Cardiff is an example of a regeneration project based within a Grade II listed building that was formerly a tram depot. It will become a 1,000-capacity live music venue with a restaurant, cocktail bar and small cinema. There will also be an art gallery, dance studios and some office space once the £4m regeneration is complete.

Incubator and accelerator programmes

Banks, alternative lenders, crowd-funding, big companies and universities are all involved in backing new economic activities in cities. www.startupbritain.org has interactive maps that plot the density and number of new businesses. LEPs (pages 44–45) are also involved, such as in the Innovation Birmingham scheme on the 14ha Aston University Science Park.

What firms are located on an innovation area such as Aston? When did they arrive, how many are employed, how have they changed the image of the place and how are they represented in the media?

Stalled Spaces Glasgow

Glasgow currently has more vacant sites than all other Scottish cities. Site plans for future development have been completed, but it can be up to 10 years before development is scheduled to start. **Stalled Spaces Glasgow** concentrates on the temporary use of stalled development vacant land and under-utilised open space, with the aim of improving community health and wellbeing. 22ha of stalled space has been used for: a green gym/play space/outdoor exercise, outdoor education, arts projects and pop-up sculpture, an urban beach and exhibitions. In this case, place and space are being used to improve lives in areas where there are environmental and socioeconomic constraints on improved health.

In Wales, the **Vibrant and Viable Places Fund** provides Welsh government money for regeneration in Bridgend, Colwyn Bay, Deeside, Holyhead, Merthyr Tydfil, Port Talbot, Newport, Pontypridd, Swansea, Pontypool and Wrexham. In addition, these funds have been granted to tackle poverty in Tredegar, Rhymney, Grangetown, Cardiff, Llanelli, Rhyl, Caernarfon and Barry.

Fieldwork

Research one of these initiatives and measure their success. Attempt to explain why they are successful or unsuccessful. If you live or study in any of these places it should be possible to evaluate the success of the projects that were funded.

Town Centre First and Great British High Street

Much city centre regeneration has focused on retailing. Town Centre First policies, initiated in 2013, are an attempt to redirect new retailing away from out-of-town sites. They require that funds are used for the regeneration of areas within the town centre. Funds may be used for developments on the edge of town centres if suitable central sites are not available. However, concentrating on the centre has been shown to have a negative effect on small corner shops and district shopping centres besides not always halting out-of-town developments. Some high streets are small, badly located and have little to no chance of competing with the internet and out-of-town retail destinations. Consequently, the policy is of little to no benefit to such places. Regeneration is unlikely and some planners recommend that the decaying main street should be transformed into housing or office space.

The annual Great British High Street competition in 2015 awarded prizes to:

- Northampton, for its innovative approach to transforming its shops and high street by bringing in residential development, developing a new cultural quarter and boosting its digital capacity
- Rotherham, for its support for start-up businesses and local retailers.

Other winners can be found on www.thegreatbritishhighstreet.co.uk.

Flagship development: the case of King's Cross (private rebranding and reimaging)

The area around King's Cross and St Pancras train stations is sandwiched between rail tracks and marshalling yards, gas holders, derelict warehousing and industrial buildings with contaminated ground, a canal and some nineteenth-century housing of poor quality. Nearby, the British Library was built and involved the eviction of 2,000 people from existing housing. Eurostar opened at St Pancras in 2007, yet the 27.1ha area north of the two stations remained undeveloped following the granting of planning permission in 2006 until 2012, when Google announced that it would move to the site.

Figure 40 shows the site, the balance of planned land uses and their locations in a mix of old refurbished building (The Granary has been converted into the home for

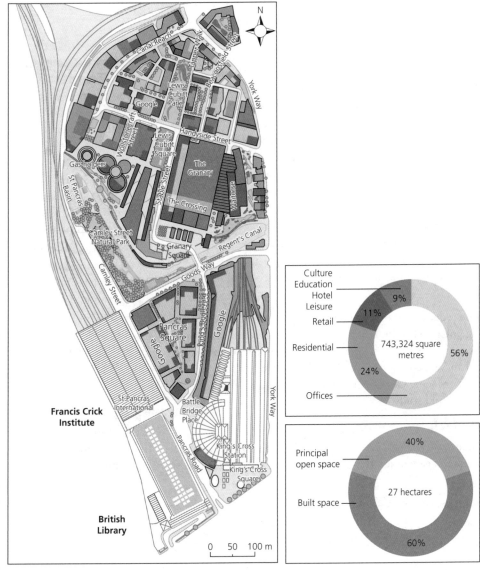

Figure 40 King's Cross regeneration area

the newly created University of the Arts). The conserved shells of the gas holders have been moved to create space for new flats. 40% of the site will be open space. The remainder will house 280,000m^2 of workspace (mainly offices) and 46,500 m^2 of education, retail and leisure uses, together with 2,000 new homes and student residences. The whole scheme is due to be completed in 2021.

The uniqueness of this redevelopment is that it is a private sector development that has taken over former public-owned land. Increasingly, large-scale redevelopment is being placed totally in the hands of private rather than public authorities because it makes raising the necessary cash much easier (*difference, globalisation, representation, risk, sustainability*).

Go to www.kingscross.co.uk/discover-kings-cross where you will find a variety of articles about the King's Cross project. This secondary information can act as a good example of an alternative place and a good point from which to re-examine your understanding of many of the key concepts. Some of the key concepts are addressed by this privately funded project, and by reading the articles you can use King's Cross to illustrate others.

- **Time:** the site has changed from industrial and transport dominance into a mixed-use site adjusted to city living and working patterns in the twenty-first century. There is a long-term historic timescale of 150 years and, for the recent developments, a timescale of decades.
- **Place:** this portion of geographic space has uniqueness and distinctiveness as a result of the way it has developed and changed. The confined site may or may not relate to other places and spaces at a range of scales. Does it have identity and if so, who is determining that identity — developers, users, residents? Does it have that layered history?
- **Identity:** how do developers, users, residents and visitors experience the development? What does the place mean to them?
- **Globalisation:** the impact of global companies such as Google on the development. The international rail links and hotels are evidence of an increasingly interconnected world.

Liverpool One (1Tha) will be redeveloped using private finance and management of the whole area, including public space for 9,000 apartments and retailing along the Mersey waterfront. The fear is that cultural facilities will be neglected as their earning potential is less. Bristol's Cabot Circus, the Canalside Birmingham and Brindley Place, and the harbour-facing Gunwharf Quays, Portsmouth, are other private regenerations that you could study.

Heritage Lottery Fund (HLF)

The fund opened in 1994 and www.hlf.org.uk gives a range of examples of the support for conservation, renovation and regeneration that the fund is providing in six fields:

1 Land and Natural Heritage
2 Museums, Libraries and Archives
3 Buildings and Monuments
4 Culture and Memories

Self-study task

You can now write your own notes on the following key concepts as illustrated by what you have read online about the King's Cross redevelopment.
— Representation
— Sustainability
— Interdependence
— Inequality
— Causality
—Attachment
— Threshold
— Risk
— Difference
— Meaning
— Resilience
— Mitigation
— The impact on people who live nearby and the new residents.

5   Industrial, Maritime and Transport

6   Community Heritage

Many of the schemes supported by the HLF involve retaining the character and *identity* of places so that they are *sustainable*. The *risks* to buildings, communities and landscapes have been *mitigated*.

> ### Fieldwork
>
> Examine how a heritage lottery fund grant has impacted on a place/s.

Perspectives of groups about identity

By the time you, the reader of this guide, are 60 years old, over 25% of people in the UK will be over 65. There will be more people over 60 than under 15. Are places considering the implications of this massive change? Some places are trying to involve all age groups, such as Edinburgh's City for All Ages to ensure full social and economic inclusion of older people. Joondalup in Australia has the Growing Old Living Dangerously (GOLD) programme to create recreational townscapes for the elderly. The World Health Organization (WHO) has listed the key dimensions of a city that is age-friendly (Figure 41). These dimensions could form the elements of an investigation into the changing nature of a place.

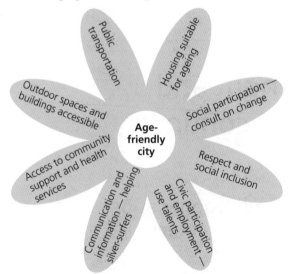

Figure 41 Aspects of age-friendly cities

For all of the policies and attempts to rebrand places, you need to ask 'who is gaining and who is losing'? This is a form of cost–benefit analysis based on welfare and is often called **welfare geography**. Is a policy favouring: (a) one group of people, (b) businesses, (c) local inhabitants, (d) young adults, (e) the wealthy investor from home or overseas, (f) the elderly, (g) those on low incomes, (h) the homeless, (i) multinational companies, or is it potentially damaging the interests of these groups?

Not all of those listed will gain or lose from a single policy intended to improve the physical and social environment of a place, but the impact on the lives of some of these groups can be examined in any reimaged and regenerated area, whether it be St David's, Grangetown, Rotherham or the Olympic Park, East London. Leicester is one city that has recently been given a chance to reimage, through becoming Premiership champions (2016), being the home city of the current World Snooker Champion (Mark Selby) and its cathedral becoming the site of burial for King Richard III's remains.

Exam tip

Have your own examples of how the identity of a neighbourhood or a place has changed, preferably taken from a place that you know well.

Self-study task

Attempt to answer the question: 'Who will gain from these events and who will not gain, or loses?'

Summary

- Rebranding and reimaging urban places is a continuous process although it has grown in importance in most developed countries.
- Promotion of places tends to be seen as business-based promotional activity.
- Lifestyle reimaging is of growing importance and is often linked to cultural regeneration of urban places.

- Local government has an important role to play in regeneration.
- Private enterprise involvement in rebranding is growing.
- The success and/or failure of all reimaging and rebranding must be judged on who gains and who loses.

■ Urban management and the challenges of continuity and change

The effects of reimaging and regeneration on the social and economic characteristics of urban places

Reimaging and regeneration is:

'an integrated set of activities that seek to reverse economic, social, environmental and physical decline to achieve lasting improvement, in areas where market forces will not do this alone without some support from government'

Welsh government

Social networks and technologies have transformed the ways in which we communicate, learn, work, consume, express emotions, relate to each other, and create and share information and knowledge. It is sometimes called a **ubiquitous commons**. Therefore, it is inevitable that the characteristics of places are perceived to be changing. Settlements have altered from being physical places on a site with links to other places, to places where data, information and knowledge is exchanged between people, while devices and data-storage points are held by organisations, companies and institutions.

Living in Safe Cities is the response of The Economist Intelligence Unit (EIU) to the challenges of modern urban life. This is a global study of 50 cities that has established the variables for deciding whether a city is secure. The index is the summary of four indices: Digital Security, Health Security, Infrastructure Safety and Personal Safety.

Fieldwork

The data used to assess if a city is safe can be found at http://safecities.economist.com/whitepapers/safe-cities-index-white-paper/. London is 18th in the ranking, Tokyo is 1st. Personal safety looks at criminal statistics, gang activity, drug use, gender safety and perceptions of safety. Use crime data or your class perceptions of safety to construct a personal safety map of a place.

Smart Cities is a movement that envisages urban managers and technology companies working together to organise urban processes more efficiently with the aim of improving quality of life. It is anticipated that IT can manage energy and water supply, transport, logistics, air and environmental quality. It comprises six key fields, which are aggregated from 90 indicators in 27 domains. Figure 42 shows the cities named as the smartest in each field in 2015 (*sustainability*).

Smart Economy (Luxembourg, Aarhus, Cork, Regensburg, Eindhoven)
Smart Mobility (Eindhoven, Salzburg, Aarhus, Luxembourg, Leicester)
Smart Environment (Umeå, Jönköping, Eskilstuna, Montpelier, Jyväskylä)
Smart Governance (Jyväskylä, Umeå, Jönköping, Odense, Aalborg)
Smart Living (Salzburg, Graz, Innsbruck, Luxembourg, Bruges)
Smart People (Eskilstuna, Tampere, Aarhus, Oulu, Umeå)

Figure 42 The six key fields of the Smart City and the smartest five cities in each field

The **Transition Towns Network** was founded in 2005. It stresses the need for community-led change in response to rising energy prices and climate change. Transition towns utilise bottom-up initiatives to address food supply, transport, energy and housing. Totnes, Devon has become one of the most advanced transition towns. Founded by community groups in 2011, Totnes Transition Network aimed to maximise local spending in the local economy (www.transitiontowntotnes.org). Of local spending on food, 66% went to the supermarkets that bought globally. By encouraging local purchasing of food, three times more jobs could be created for the same spending on food. The local multiplier effect has been calculated to show that every £1 spent in local suppliers generated spending of £1.76 in the local economy, compared with only 36p if the same £1 was spent in a supermarket. Also, by developing a local currency (the Totnes £) local spending is encouraged. (Brixton, Bristol, Lewes and Stroud also have their own currency) (*sustainability*).

Fieldwork

One challenge that the *Grimsey Review* identified is how to deal with vacant floors above shops in town centres. Carry out a survey of the upper storeys that are out of use. Where are they in the central retail area?

Ongoing challenges in urban places with regeneration/rebranding

Challenges where regeneration/rebranding are absent or have failed

In 2014, Hall identified five twenty-first-century challenges for urban areas in the UK:

1 **Rebalancing our urban economies:** Figure 43 shows how some places have embraced the new economies while others lag behind.

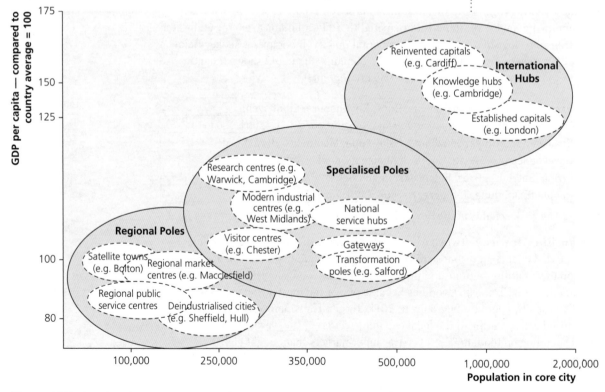

Figure 43 Embracing the new economies (Hall's categorisation of places)

2 **Building new homes:** where should new homes be built, and for whom? How do we secure brownfield land for homes? Bristol is under-supplied with homes. In 2013, the Bristol Homes Commission identified sites that best meet needs through freeing up land used by the council and by targeting 'greyfield' land, i.e. underused public amenity land such as over-large car parks close to existing neighbourhoods.

3 **Linking people and places:** this challenge arises because many places have developed over a long time. Therefore, the public transport system linking people and workplace, often built over a century ago, needs updating to cater for the new work patterns and workplaces (e.g. Elizabeth Line/Crossrail). The Armitt Review 2013 examined the British transport infrastructure and recommended that transport planning must meet the needs of people and cover appropriate economic areas. The various authorities concerned with transport should coordinate their activities, creating integrated transport authorities, as is the case in London (TfL).

   a Trams were abolished but today, new tramways are an efficient transport system in Manchester, Sheffield and Croydon. With a few exceptions, cities in the UK have not been built for the car or indeed the bicycle.

   b Adjusting roads to cope with modern patterns of workplaces and the volume of vehicles on the road is a challenge.

   c Dutch cities and Copenhagen are among a few cities that have really embraced the bicycle. In the UK, 43% of the lowest income households and 66% of those on Job Seeker's Allowance do not have access to a car. If they are to benefit from city centre job growth there must be adequate public transport.

4 **Living within finite resources:** (energy issues are covered by the Component 3 option, Energy challenges and dilemmas). This sustainable living challenge will have to address: a) sustainable energy, b) sustainable housing, c) sustainable waste management, d) sustainable water supply and e) sustainable food supplies. Urbanisation is greedy and dirty. City inhabitants consume 75% of the planet's natural resources.

5 **Fixing broken machinery:** does the planning system work? The 2015 Budget in the UK allocated £40m to 'the Internet of Things', which will make places smarter and more dependent on smart technologies (*sustainability*).

The property development industry and investors and providers of finance characterise city challenges differently because they see places as economic units that both generate and consume money. In 2012, the *Financial Times* reported that places with few new start-up businesses needed initiatives to enhance their economic base. Belfast, Sunderland, Stoke-on-Trent, Mansfield, Swansea, Hull, Dundee, Barnsley, Plymouth and Wakefield were all identified as problem places, and in the cases of Sunderland, Grimsby, Stoke and Swansea, these were places where many businesses were started, but more failed than succeeded. These are the cities most affected by deindustrialisation. The property development company Jones Lang LaSalle (JLL) identified three types of city based on the potential performance of the property market (Table 21). The table also lists the buoyant, stable and struggling cities identified by the research group, Centre for Cities (it excludes the largest cities).

Table 21 City typologies after Jones Lang LaSalle and the Centre for Cities

Jones Lang LaSalle		
Growth leaders	**Potential performers**	**Awaiting lift-off**
Brighton	Bournemouth	Bedford
Coventry	Cardiff	Leicester
Derby	Luton	Liverpool
Portsmouth	Northampton	Plymouth
Reading	Oxford	Sheffield
Solihull	Peterborough	Swansea
Swindon	Southampton	York
	Warrington	
The Centre for Cities		
Buoyant cities	**Stable cities**	**Struggling cities**
London	Bournemouth	Bolton
Milton Keynes	Portsmouth	Barnsley
Cambridge	Northampton	Middlesbrough
Reading	Southampton	Hull
Crawley	York	Blackburn
Oxford	Leeds	Birkenhead
Aldershot	Peterborough	Burnley
Bristol	Preston	Stoke-on-Trent

All of these typologies affect both the place and the people who live there. Do these places represent themselves in the same way? Is the age structure the same or are the struggling cities older and growing more slowly? Will the middle-aged person in a struggling city view their home place in the same way as a similarly aged person in a stable or buoyant city?

In 2014, the Royal Town Planning Institute (RTPI) noted that most governmental documents that examined the future for cities did not contain maps and, therefore, lacked an awareness of space and place. As a consequence, policies may not recognise the interconnections and interdependence between places and the impact of decisions on places and the people who live in them.

The New Cities Foundation (www.newcitiesfoundation.org) has a range of case studies that suggest how people and places can respond to the challenges of the twenty-first century.

Challenges where there is overheating

Overheating is a term taken from economics that describes an area where increased demand (in our case, for housing and office space) results in rising prices rather than increased output. London is the classic geographical case of a city with the potential to overheat. There are 10 times per annum more new jobs in London than in any other city in the UK. Some drivers of overheating are:

■ **New twenty-first-century employers:** in 2015, the Francis Crick Institute, King's Cross, opened in London, becoming the biggest biomedical research centre in the world (Figure 40). It will employ 1,500 highly qualified staff due to

Knowledge check 16

Outline the benefits and problems of using the upper floors above shops.

Knowledge check 17

'Any city however small, is in fact divided into two: one the city of the poor, the other of the rich.'

Plato's *Republic*, 360 BC

How far is this true today? Write a plan for your 30-minute essay.

Exam tip

Always plan any piece of prose, even for the mini-essays, during the exam. If you do not finish the essay, the examiner still has the plan to assess.

(a) expertise in the universities, (b) the expertise and patient variety in London hospitals, (c) the appeal of London as a global city for young scientists and (d) the financial and legal expertise needed to support the commercialisation of research. This is just one example of the quaternary industry driving demand for space.

- **Brownfield land:** 10.1ha of land at White City will soon become the site for another Imperial College research hub. However, finding sites for the ambitions of others is difficult. Shoreditch, Hackney, Stratford and south of the Thames are being rapidly developed for new activities.

Drawbacks

- **Housing:** a potential drawback of growth is housing for the 2,000 new people who arrive in London every eight days; not all of these are highly qualified, but many existing residents in some areas are not. 12% of Londoners live in overcrowded conditions. London needs 42,000 new homes a year for a decade, not only for the increasing workforce but because the size of households is rising from 2.35 in 2001 to 2.47 in 2011. House prices have been rising at up to 10% a year, whereas outside of London the rise is 3.1%. Therefore, to get adequate housing, some are being forced to commute larger distances from the South East and beyond. The processes outlined here of housing shortages and rapidly rising prices, together with foreign investors buying up property as an investment, have been labelled 'plutocratisation'.

- **Transport infrastructure:** this is under strain, even with the building of Crossrail and the completion of London Overground Orbirail (orbital railway). The pressure to expand airport capacity is yet another consequence of the heat of the London economy and the wealth of its society. Projects such as Crossrail are leading to further house price increases close to the stations on the line.

- A further response to the overheated economy is to **increase diversity** by enabling women to take a greater proportion of senior posts rather than the 6% on executive and board positions in 2015.

> 'Diversity means businesses employ a true meritocracy, so that the best succeed, regardless of gender, race, sexuality or nationality.'
>
> Fiona Woolf, Lord Mayor of London, 2013

Yet still London contains some of the most deprived areas in the UK.

- **Brain drain:** some are of the opinion that overheating in London draws talent away from the rest of the country, and London-based firms dominate the economy of cities beyond the capital. As a consequence, other cities underperform. The 'metropolitan elite' is often criticised in the media, which reflects concerns that London is overheating economically, politically and socially (*difference, inequality, resilience, risk*).

- **Fast Growth Cities** are those that perform well on many indicators, and include Cambridge, Milton Keynes, Norwich, Oxford and Swindon. Their economies are strong and productive, generating over £3,000/worker. These places are attractive as places to live. However, the downsides are transport congestion, shortages of housing, which can be unaffordable, and the problem of those with no qualifications who are unable to find jobs in cities demanding high-level skills.

Exam tip

Have other examples of named companies that are expanding and contributing to overheating. It often pays to have two examples, because that shows breadth of knowledge.

> **Self-study task**
>
> The points above are made about London and Cambridge. To what extent do these factors apply to your home urban area? Are similar factors affecting other areas that are overheating such as San Francisco and Silicon Valley?

Challenges of segregation and inequality

A characteristic of cities in the USA in the twentieth century has been growing segregation, a feature that is increasingly evident in British cities. The modern large city is marked by increasingly sharp inequalities aided by the high earnings of those in the quaternary sector and legal services. The inequality grows with city size. In the 1840s, Engels noted segregation in the industrial UK in Manchester, while Disraeli identified the two nations: the rich and the poor. Spatial segregation is a process over time that involves:

- **concentration:** the increasing juxtaposition of similar social and racial groups
- **invasion:** the migration of similar groups into an area
- **succession:** the replacement of one group by an incoming group, e.g. Somalis replacing Afro-Caribbeans
- **flight:** often referred to as white flight due to the departure of the former inhabitants of an area. Between 2001 and 2011, according to the research group Demos, over 620,000 British people left London when the population rose by over a million.

Types of segregation

- **Ethnic:** the concentration of minority ethnic groups, e.g. multi-racial population in the Lozells area of Birmingham; Bangladeshis in Tower Hamlets, London.
- **Class:** the concentration of particular earning and employment groups.
- **Life cycle:** the grouping of people at stages of their lives into specific areas. In London, Hoxton and Clapham have above average concentrations of single people whereas Richmond-upon-Thames has an above average share of older people.
- **Lifestyle:** could be, for example, student areas, or gay and lesbian districts such as Castro, San Francisco and Canal Street, Manchester.
- **Linguistic:** often related to the types above, e.g. some Muslim women in the UK cannot speak the English language.
- **Religious:** concentration of adherents to a religion over time, e.g. Belfast.

These examples are all taken from Cheshire & Umberti (2014) *London: The Informational Capital* (Particular Books), which contains many maps of various types of segregation.

Factors causing residential segregation

- **Ability to pay for housing, whether to buy or let:** this results from inequalities in income. According to the Joseph Rowntree Foundation, income inequality is highest in London but also high in other towns and cities, e.g. Reading, Bracknell, Guildford, Watford.
- **Availability of housing:** a lack of starter homes for young persons or social housing/housing association properties for low-income households.

- **Gatekeepers:** landlords, estate agents, banks, mortgage companies and 'the bank of Mum and Dad'. By raising rents, often on an annual basis, landlords can re-engineer the social make-up of a neighbourhood. Rents are set at levels determined by demand but also at levels that either exclude or include certain social groups. Mortgages are awarded on the basis of ability to pay both the deposit and the subsequent monthly repayments. More affluent parents can assist with deposits that might enable their children to live in the more desirable areas or have a foot on the ladder towards living in the most suitable neighbourhood for their lifestyle.
- **Demand for housing:** in some places, this is caused by gentrification that pushes, for example, Londoners to the outer boroughs and beyond. Overseas investors are also raising the level of demand in London, yet leaving expensive property empty.
- **Threat hypothesis:** segregation is stimulated by perceived and actual threats to the way of life. Besides perceived social threats, the perceived danger of crime often portrayed by the media, such as riots, will deter some people and attract those who need lower housing costs.
- **Marginalisation of workers:** especially in manufacturing due to deindustrialisation and competition with both the more educated and other ethnic groups, who may be immigrants, for new jobs.
- **Government policies towards housing immigrants:** refugees and asylum seekers, e.g. Kosovans in Croydon and Somalis in Cardiff. There are also government-defined dispersal areas for asylum seekers that lead to the growth of refugee communities in places such as Bolton, Portsmouth, Rotherham and Swansea.
- **Past government policies:** especially the building of council estates, now called social housing, which pushed lower income households on to peripheral estates. Despite the 'right-to-buy' initiative, many of these areas are still marginalised.
- **Immigrant groups:** often congregate in the area in which they first arrived before spreading to other areas over time. A former Welsh chapel on the Mile End Road, E1 is a representation of a nineteenth-century cluster of migrants from Wales. Bangladeshis cluster in Tower Hamlets, which has traditionally been the first home for these migrant communities. Family and friends come to the same neighbourhood, often referred to as chain migration.
- **Affluent households:** areas that attract more affluent people; the greater the wealth of the city expressed as GDP per capita, the more affluent the areas present.
- **Property development industry:** creates fear by building gated and walled developments.
- **Unforeseen consequences of past 'social' policies:** the following points are made by Professor Danny Dorling of Oxford University. In the second part of the twentieth century a series of policies to address inequalities have given rise to greater inequality and segregation. Educational reforms in the twentieth century have led to a greater body of well-qualified people, both male and female, and to them being segregated by educational outcome as a new elite. In the 1960s, full employment meant that all had their basic needs satisfied. However, full employment led to the wages of those in the worst jobs declining while those in the better positions saw salaries rising. The consequence was the beginnings of social exclusion as the rich bought more whereas those in poverty were excluded from being consumers.

Prejudice against the less fortunate by birth, ability, home location and place in the labour market rose, thus reinforcing segregation. Affluence has led to greed for ever higher salaries to enable people to live a life that equates with their status as, for example, a banker or lawyer wishing to live in the most desirable suburbs of a city. The unfortunate by-product of these trends is that there are those in a state of despair who might live in overcrowded and possibly insanitary conditions in older buildings. Most segregated are the homeless street dwellers and those who depend on food banks.

Self-study task

Investigate the relative importance of these factors in your home town. Use the 2011 census ward data, which will give you valuable data on the social composition of areas.

How can segregation and inequality be reduced in places?

'Geographically, with each year that passes, where you live becomes more important.'

Danny Dorling, *Injustice*, 2010

Income and wealth inequality was noted in the specialised concepts as 'the greatest threat to society today' and a dominant cause of segregation. Segregation emphasises differences between places at the neighbourhood and local scales. People within areas that are different can and do form attachments to the area and become resilient when the status quo is threatened. Therefore, policies to address segregation involve risk and mitigation, and are the responsibility of local and national governments that are politically motivated.

One consequence is that policies and outcomes for localities will vary according to the political ideology of the decision-makers in government and/or private companies at the time of implementation. The building of social housing estates in the last century segregated some people to the fringe and others to high-rise blocks in the inner city. Both of these solutions have resulted in problems that were manifested by, for example, riots in Tottenham and the Parisian *banlieue* (suburbs) of Grigny. The twenty-first-century response is often to tear down the inner city towers and replace them with terraces, whose inhabitants have the right to buy. How can we alleviate the problems related to segregation and inequality? The following is a list of potential solutions (note: the list is not in any particular order).

1 Policies that tackle the fact that as affluence grows more people are living in poverty.

2 Planning policies that demand that new developments have a mix of housing, including social housing and 'starter homes'.

3 **Contact hypothesis** states that areas with greater diversity associated with more inter-ethnic contact lowers ethnic animosity, whereas 'white' neighbourhoods with little diversity are unaffected.

4 Laws to stop discrimination in the rental market, which was prevalent in the past when signs on doors stated who would not be offered the accommodation to rent (signs in the 1960s drew attention to nationality and skin colour).

5 Benefits policies were originally designed to reduce inequality.

Self-study task

Summative

Figure 44 is a rework of Robson's 1975 model of urban social areas to schematise the structure of urban places today. To enable you to summarise your learning, try to list the challenges that are faced by each of the zones of this mythical urban area. How are these areas represented, how are they changing and what are the policies and pressures leading to change?

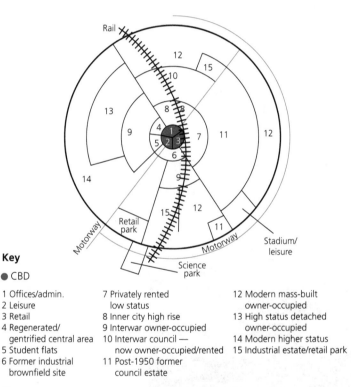

Key

● CBD

1 Offices/admin.
2 Leisure
3 Retail
4 Regenerated/ gentrified central area
5 Student flats
6 Former industrial brownfield site

7 Privately rented low status
8 Inner city high rise
9 Interwar owner-occupied
10 Interwar council — now owner-occupied/rented
11 Post-1950 former council estate

12 Modern mass-built owner-occupied
13 High status detached owner-occupied
14 Modern higher status
15 Industrial estate/retail park

Figure 44 The structure of a twenty-first century urban area

Exam tip

Please do not use or refer to the Burgess model of urban structure because it is almost a century old.

Summary

- Movements such as Safe Cities and the Transition Towns Network are attempts to alter the social and economic life of urban places.
- Challenges remain despite the efforts of those who rebrand and reimage places.
- Over-successful towns and cities have challenges that result from overheating of economic activity and consequent social change.

- Spatial segregation and inequalities have risen alongside the economic success of urban places.
- Measures to reduce inequalities and spatial segregation are dependent on governmental policies, and they often have unintended effects.
- Every area of a city faces challenges resulting from its evolution over time, which can be studied in the field.

Questions & Answers

About this section

The questions below are typical of the style and structure that you can expect to see in the actual exam papers. Each question is followed by examiner comments, which offer some guidance on question interpretation. For the AS questions, the number of lines that would be given in the exam answer booklet are provided as an indication of the level of detail required. Student responses are also provided, with detailed examiner comments for each answer, to indicate the strengths and weaknesses of the answer and the number of marks that would be awarded. A final summary comment is also provided, giving the total mark and grade standard.

When the examiners read your work they will have a small grid telling them the maximum marks for each Assessment Objective (AO) (page 7). In the example questions that follow, this grid has been placed after each question part. The official mark scheme will include indications of the contents, marking guidance and, for mark totals in excess of 5, marks bands. One cannot say what grade any of these answers will obtain because, at the time of writing, boundaries have not been decided.

Question 1

 This question follows the format for the Eduqas A-level short structured questions. You have 15 minutes to read and answer the question. It uses a photographic source to test your knowledge of how the identity of places is interpreted and boosted.

Figure 1

(a) i What do geographers understand by the identity of a place? (2 marks)

What do geographers understand by the identity of a place?	AO1	AO2.1a	AO2.1b	AO2.1c	AO3.1	AO3.2	Total
	2						2

ii Describe the place shown in Figure 1 in terms of its identity. (5 marks)

Describe the place shown on Plate 1 in terms of its identity.	AO1	AO2.1a	AO2.1b	AO2.1c	AO3.1	AO3.2	Total
					5		5

(b) How might the local council and tourist board represent this place? (6 marks)

How might the local council and tourist board represent this place?	AO1	AO2.1a	AO2.1b	AO2.1c	AO3.1	AO3.2	Total
	6						6

Student A

(a) i Identity is what a place means to a person or group. It can be different for different people.

🅔 **2/2 marks awarded.** This answer is complete and would gain 2 marks.

ii The place might be a village because there appears to be open space across the top of the photo. There seem to be some shop fronts around the central open area where cars are parked. This suggests that it is a small town. There is some industry at the top alongside the river.

🅔 **4/5 marks awarded.** The place is described and given an identity using the resource. It would gain top band (4–5 marks) but it lacks any reference to the built identity old buildings and so is probably 4 marks.

(b) The council as a formal agency might represent this place as a quiet village with facilities such as the shops and church for the population. They might say that parking is easy as you can see in the centre. The tourist board may stress boat hire from the premises at the top. It is possible that one of the buildings in the centre is a hotel so there is somewhere to stay. People may like to visit the church and other tourist sites. This could be presented online.

🅔 **5/6 marks awarded.** There is a slight slip because the student has reverted to calling it a village. There is recognition of different ways of representing a place and a mention of representing the place in the media, although not in e.g. tourist literature. The answer is on the cusp of top and middle bands (4–5 marks) but it has enough understanding of representation to gain the top band.

🅔 **Total score: 11/13 marks awarded**

Student B

(a) i   People identify things and places.

🅔 **1/2 marks awarded.** The student recognises that identity is related to people and places but the answer lacks clarity.

ii   The photo shows a village with old houses and a church grouped round what was the village green until it became a car park. There is a lot of green space and a church near the centre. It is winter and there is a river.

🅔 **2/5 marks awarded.** There are some observations based on the photo without any attempt to locate them other than assuming that the marker knows where he is describing. It is a partially developed description of the place's identity and would only gain the middle band marks.

(b) The tourist board and council will have a website where they advertise the village. They will say that it is pretty, has parking and old buildings and a church. Tourist boards often have leaflets that they can send out with more photos of e.g. the church and comments from visitors. They will make the place sound better than it is to attract people to come to the village.

🅔 **3/6 marks awarded.** This answer displays some understanding of the role of agencies. Otherwise, it lacks detail on how place can be represented so that it attracts people. It is slightly disorganised and in need of support, yet is perceptive about why the council might want people to come. It is just a middle band answer.

🅔 **Total score: 6/13 marks awarded**

Question 2

ⓔ This question follows one of the formats for the Eduqas AS paper. You have 15 minutes to read and answer the question. It tests your ability to interpret and explain a graph, and the essay follows the same theme of employment.

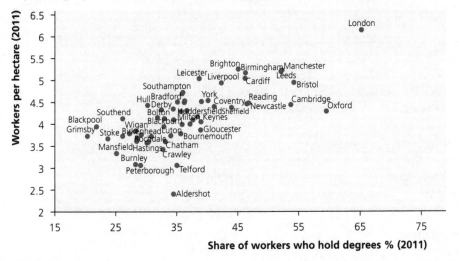

Figure 2

(a) i Figure 2 shows the density of workers and share of graduates in English and Welsh city centres in 2011.

Describe the pattern shown on the graph. (3 marks)

Describe the pattern shown on the graph.	AO1	AO2.1a	AO2.1b	AO2.1c	AO3.1	AO3.2	Total
					3		**3**

ii What factors might explain the relationship shown in Figure 2? (4 marks)

What factors might explain the relationship shown in Figure 2?	AO1	AO2.1a	AO2.1b	AO2.1c	AO3.1	AO3.2	Total
	4						**4**

(b) Describe and explain recent changes to the central areas of cities in the UK. (13 marks)

ⓔ Within your answer to question (b), you are required to demonstrate your ability to develop a sustained line of reasoning that is coherent, relevant, substantiated and logically structured.

Describe and explain recent changes to the central areas of cities in the UK.	A01	A02.1a	A02.1b	A02.1c	A03.1	A03.2	Total
	7			6			13

Student A

(a) i   The graph shows workers per hectare and the share of those who hold a degree. Not all the dots are named. London has the highest of both and Aldershot is different because it is outside the rest.

🅮 **1/3 marks awarded.** The first sentence is just a copy of the two axes and the second sentence is irrelevant. The information on London is correct. The information about Aldershot should have stated that it is an outlier. The marker would be looking for more descriptive statements using data from the graph.

ii   London is a major place for work and its industries attract graduates. The next four cities all have universities so you would expect there to be graduates. Grimsby and Mansfield do not have universities, I think, so that is why they are to the left. Some places are big and others are small. Cardiff is the capital of Wales.

🅮 **2/4 marks awarded.** This answer gives clues to the reasons but never really shows that the student understands the reasons fully. The statement on London is correct although it would have helped to mention the types of industry. The statements on universities are again correct, despite being limited to six of the named cities. The answer needed to say why Cardiff is highly placed on both variables so once again it is a half-truth rather than a full explanation. All of these elements add up to 2 marks.

(b)   I will list the changes that have taken place in Southampton and I will explain why there was change.

The first change has been the WestQuay centre, which is a large covered centre that includes lots of shops, especially women's shops, John Lewis and lots of car parking. Across the road from it are other shops such as IKEA, Halfords and JD Sports. All of this is next to the High Street called Above Bar. This has been done to make the city centre more attractive because people were not coming to it and staying at the out-of-town centres such as Hedge End.

The second change has been the use of parts of the centre for markets, which I looked at for fieldwork. There are Farmer's Markets, a general market and a specialist market. These all attract people who live in the city to come to the centre.

The third change has been more leisure. New hotels, clubs and the football ground occupy sites just outside of the centre and the hotels are for those staying before going on a cruise.

Finally, student hostels have been built for both universities in the centre. Some include gyms. These have been built because the numbers of students have grown and they like being in the middle of a city rather than in victorian housing.

It can be seen that shopping, markets, leisure and students have changed Southampton.

ⓔ This essay will have 2 marks, one for each AO. These marks will be in bands out of 7 and 6 respectively.

ⓔ 8/13 marks awarded.

AO1 Demonstrates knowledge and understanding of changes in city centres and the causes of change.

Although only one city has been described, the answer appears to have been based on some fieldwork. It demonstrates partial knowledge with some detail and variable understanding of changes in a city centre. Four changes are discussed, three (retailing) in more detail. The answer is certainly at the top of band 2 and fringing band 3 — 4/5 marks.

Applies (AO2.1c) to appraise through assessing the relative explanations for changes and their importance relative to one another and different places.

The answer applies knowledge and understanding through a partial explanation of different types of change, supported by some appropriate evidence but without development of the points in all of the paragraphs. This is characteristic of the middle band (2) and would gain 4 marks.

ⓔ **Total score: 11/20 marks awarded**

Student B

(a) i The graph shows that London is an exception or outlier on both scales. The larger the city the more workers per ha and more graduates. Many of these have universities in them e.g. Liverpool and Oxford. Those cities that have high percentages are those where the tertiary and quaternary industries dominate whereas those with the lower percentage are often places where deindustrialisation has occurred.

ⓔ 3/3 marks awarded. Despite the answer moving into answering (aii) here, the student does note the outlier and size.

> ii As I said in the other answer, many of the cities have universities and are the location of modern jobs. Cambridge has many biotech jobs and London is the focus for many tech companies, finance and creative work such as TV. Tech work is growing fast in all cities in the upper half whereas those with fewer graduates have lost activities such as fishing in Grimsby and cotton in Burnley.

ⓔ 4/4 marks awarded. This response does develop points about the type of employment and the role of universities. The examiner accepted the statements given in (ai) because the student acknowledged them. There is some support using vague place knowledge.

> **(b)** City centres are changing in almost all urban areas but the rate and type of change does differ. I have defined the city centre as both the CBD and the areas around it.
>
> People are moving back into city centres, which is called reurbanisation. Many new housing developments are being built near to the centre or on former industrial or dock land. These developments such as Cardiff Bay are for the young and well-off and is called gentrification.
>
> Many city centres are being redeveloped especially for retailing such as the Arndale centre in Manchester and St David's 2 in Cardiff. This is because the city council wants to keep the centre attractive to people. Old offices of banks are being redeveloped as shops and restaurants.
>
> Leisure districts have developed in city centres because people have money to spend and want to go clubbing. The Millennium Stadium in Cardiff is the ultimate leisure venue next to the city centre and nearby are the clubs and pubs of Market Street.
>
> Some cities have developed office districts to provide modern employment such as Croydon and Bournemouth.
>
> Streets have been pedestrianised and artworks and fountains placed in some streets. Some streets have declined and only have loan shops and betting shops.

ⓔ This essay will have 2 marks, one for each AO. These marks will be in bands out of 7 and 6 respectively.

ⓔ 10/13 marks awarded.

AO1 Demonstrates knowledge and understanding of changes in city centres and the causes of change.

The answer does demonstrate a knowledge of changes in retailing — which is mentioned twice — leisure, offices and housing. It demonstrates understanding of the reasons for some of the changes, although it is rushed towards the end and lacks support or reasons. It does identify a range of cities. Knowledge is accurate and terms are used at the start. It is worth 6 marks.

Applies (AO2.1c) to appraise through assessing the relative explanations for changes and their importance relative to one another and different places.

The answer begins with some reasonable explanations but time constraints have resulted in a rush at the end, with nothing drawing the essay to a conclusion. There are some partially developed arguments and all change seems to be the same because there is no attempt to measure the relative impact. These are characteristic of band 2 and so it is worth 4 marks.

ⓔ Total score: 17/20 marks awarded

Question 3

ⓔ This question follows the format for the WJEC AS paper. You have 18 minutes to read and answer the question. This style of question, which tests statistics, can also appear on both the Eduqas A-level and AS papers.

In a study of deprivation in 33 wards of a Welsh city it was hypothesised: (a) that unemployment would decline with distance from the centre and (b) areas with high unemployment would also be areas where a high proportion of the population had no qualifications. A Spearman rank (Rs) was used to test these hypotheses. The result for (a) was 0.388 and (b) 0.8264.

(a) i What do the test results state about the two hypotheses? (2 marks)

What do the test results state about the two hypotheses?	AO1	AO2.1a	AO2.1b	AO2.1c	AO3.1	AO3.2	Total
						2	2

ii Figure 3 is a scatter plot of the relationship between Distance from the same city centre and Average income per week of the working population in the ward.
Suggest how the identities of the wards marked X might differ between themselves and contrast with the wards marked Y. (3 marks)

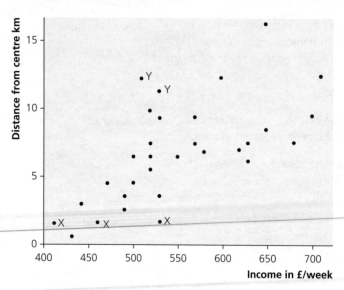

Figure 3 Distance from city centre and average weekly income

Suggest how the identities of the wards marked X might differ between themselves and contrast with the wards marked Y.	AO1	AO2.1a	AO2.1b	AO2.1c	AO3.1	AO3.2	Total
	3						3

(b) Assess the impact of fast growing city economies on the lives of people. (11 marks)

Assess the impact of fast growing city economies on the lives of people	AO1	AO2.1a	AO2.1b	AO2.1c	AO3.1	AO3.2	Total
	6			5			11

Student A

(a) i The result for (a) tells me that the relationship is not strong and therefore unemployment does not decline with distance. Whereas there is a strong relationship between unemployment and no qualifications. Wards with high unemployment are more likely to have people with no qualifications.

ⓔ **2/2 marks awarded.** This is a full answer and should gain full marks.

ii The wards marked X are all close to the city centre and one has far higher incomes, which may mean that the place is a gentrified ward of better housing. Those marked Y have incomes of less or the same as the gentrified area. They are probably outer suburban areas of substantial housing possibly dating from mid-twentieth century.

ⓔ **3/3 marks awarded.** Identifies the characteristics of both sets of areas in terms of inhabitants in the wards and a slight bit about the buildings, which might give the areas identity.

> **(b)** I am going to define a fast growing city as one where there are many new jobs in the tech industry. I will look at the costs and benifits of fast growth.
>
> Tech industries in big cities attract young workers because they pay high wages. The workers will be mainly graduates from universities. This is the case in London where in Shoreditch and Canary Wharf there are many tech industries including software design and banking. This benifits the young workers who can then use the bars and clubs in the area. So more people get work.
>
> Because so many young people are moving to these areas house rents and prices go up because there are not enough houses for them. Some will have to move away to get housing and commute from Essex. Higher house rents mean that the unqualified people who lived here in the last century can no longer afford the rents and have to go to cheaper areas outside of London. The housing that is being built is too expensive.
>
> If people have to commute there will be more traffic congestion and crowded trains. Crossrail is being built to try to ease congestion, as is the London Overground. More buildings are being regenerated and others are being pulled down to make way for more offices. Some of these might have been the homes of the old working population. Therefore fast growing economies have both good and bad effects.

ⓔ **5/11 marks awarded.**

AO1 Demonstrates knowledge and understanding of fast-growing city economies and the impact on people.

The student has tried to give the essay structure with an introduction, content and conclusion. It is all rather deliberate, displaying some knowledge that is mainly based on London. The knowledge is superficial and the examples rather generalised and not fully developed. It is better on the costs. Understanding is partial, probably because the level of language is unsophisticated, including spelling errors. It is a band 2 answer gaining 4 marks.

Applies AO2.1c to assess the relative impacts, both positive and negative on groups of people.

There is not much assessment of the costs and benefits, which are in a descriptive list. Impacts are noted but they really needed the student to say what the impact meant for the groups affected. It is worth 2 marks.

A mid-range mark is achieved because of the ability to interpret data.

ⓔ **Total score: 11/16 marks awarded**

Questions & Answers

(a) i Unemployment and qualifications are linked.

e **1/2 marks awarded.** This brief statement only deals with one hypothesis and can only gain 1 mark.

ii The X areas are identified as inner city areas of older housing where lower income people live, whereas the Y areas are further out and are suburbs.

e **2/3 marks awarded.** Two basic statements that can gain a mark apiece.

(b) Fast-growing cities are places such as Cambridge, London and Oxford, are the economically successful cities of the twenty-first century where knowledge-based employment is strong. People are affected both positively and negatively both in those places and beyond.

These cities have attracted modern industries such as biotech in Cambridge, digital media in Shoreditch, London. In Swindon almost 40% of the workforce is in managerial and professional groups. Outside of London places such as Swindon, Oxford and Milton Keynes all have good transport links to London. These cities identify themselves on the quality of life that can be achieved which attracts younger, highly qualified people to work and live in them. Earnings are high, in Swindon workers add over £58,000 to the economy and that is one-third higher than a decade ago. Success brings more new companies and expansion so attracting more people. As a result Swindon's population has grown by almost 16% since 2004.

Success brings challenges for people. House building has not kept pace with the increase in households and so prices have risen although not as fast as nearby Oxford where a green belt constrains growth. To obtain affordable homes to buy or let some of the new population is living around Cricklade and Lyneham and commuting to work. This issue is far worse in both Oxford and Cambridge where many commute from 15 miles away. Commuting leads to congestion and increased pollution that may affect health of people, particularly those living near main routes.

As prices rise, those on low incomes and who rent their house may be forced to leave. This might deprive Swindon of workers in lower skilled jobs and increase their costs of getting to work.

In conclusion, people are affected by fast growing cities but on balance more people gain than lose.

e **11/11 marks awarded.**

AO1 Demonstrates knowledge and understanding of fast growing city economies and the impact on people.

The answer shows that the student has made good use of their home place and has contrasted it with other places within the essay. Knowledge is good and backed up by statistics that must have come from either fieldwork or secondary sources. AO1 is worth 7 marks, because there is little else that could be achieved in the time.

Applies AO2.1c to assess the relative impacts, both positive and negative on groups of people.

There is a statement in the conclusion that tries to assess the overall impact. Likewise the first sentence of the third paragraph is trying to provide assessment. Perhaps more assessment could have been used as the essay went along. Is there enough about people who are mentioned but only as broad categories? Nevertheless, this is a top band response worth 5 marks.

This question relied on a good essay, which makes up for weaker understanding of the data.

ⓔ **Total score: 14/16 marks awarded**

Question 4

ⓔ **This question follows the format for the Eduqas A-level extended response question, which will be questions 11 and 12 in the actual examination. You have 20 minutes to read the question, plan and write the essay.**

To what extent are rural settlements no longer villages, hamlets and farms serving a rural economy?

(15 marks)

To what extent are rural settlements no longer villages, hamlets and farms serving a rural economy?	AO1	AO2.1a	AO2.1b	AO2.1c	AO3.1	AO3.2	Total
	10			5			15

Student A

Villages are changing because of counter-urbanisation, which is the movement of people from towns to villages.

People want to live in the countryside because it is more pleasant than living in congested towns, which have higher crime, more pollution and less open space. So people move to villages where the environment is less polluted and more pleasant. Many of these people move just before retirement or continue to commute back to the town where they work.

People no longer work in agriculture or fishing because of the EU quotas and because of mechanisation of farming. Many farms now offer tourist accommodation and some have other activities such as a farm shop. Barns have been sold off for offices or for housing conversions.

ⓔ 5/15 marks awarded.

AO1 Demonstrates knowledge and understanding of change in rural areas.

The student wanted an essay on counter-urbanisation. It does include knowledge, which is relevant but poorly applied to the question. The first paragraph is all about counter-urbanisation and is relevant. The next paragraph does mention four possible reasons for change but none are developed. It is limited knowledge and understanding of changes with exemplification only applied to counter-urbanisation. There is no place knowledge. Therefore, this is in the bottom band and would be awarded 3 marks.

Applies AO2.1c to evaluate the relative impacts of change on rural settlements and their people.

'To what extent' requires some evaluation of the reasons for change and the essay only states reasons, although possibly implying some evaluation by giving prominence to counter-urbanisation. Therefore, there is limited evaluation. There is some structure to the answer. The effect of change on some people is noted but not investigated in any depth. Therefore, this might creep into the middle band and gain 2 marks.

> ### Student B
>
> I have looked at how two villages in Powys have changed in recent years. Secondary data was difficult to find because the villages are part of larger statistical units. I will use these villages to show what changes have taken place.
>
> Villages, hamlets and farms were places where people worked in agriculture and in some of them mining and forestry. The number employed in agriculture has declined, although with 22% employed in it in Llansilin, it seems quite high still, but this is only 140 people, some of whom are on family farms where everyone works. The populations are getting older with over half of the population of Llansilin over 45. The image of Llansilin was represented in 1980s tourist literature from the AA as neat whitewashed cottages with a splash of colour along a main street past the church to a pub. It was used in films because of its traditional Welsh appearance.
>
> However, villages are changing while trying to keep the past identity. Meifod, which was also described as neat stone buildings, has been the venue for cultural events such as the 2015 Welsh Eisteddfod, which attracted 150,000 visitors = cultural boosting of the village. Farm barns are being sold for barn conversions for second homes, cottages to rent and retirement. Another house is being sold with the potential to be a B&B. Therefore the area is becoming socially different, with outsiders coming in. A former chapel in Llansilin has been converted into a house.
>
> In order to retain some rural services Llansilin has opened a community shop and post office in a former chapel.

Some of the people work in Welshpool and Oswestry and even commute to Shrewsbury. These people are those described as counter-urbanisation. A few have set up their own businesses from home and have brought tertiary industry to the villages.

Villages have changed from being primary places to more diverse places trying to hold on to their former identity. It depends on the place when trying to say what reason is more important.

ⓔ 13/15 marks awarded.

AO1 Demonstrates knowledge and understanding of change in rural areas.

It would appear that the student has studied two villages, perhaps because these are in the home area, a requirement of the specification. There is knowledge based on secondary sources. The answer demonstrates awareness of three key concepts: identity, representation and place, and has accurate knowledge about changes in two places. This is a top-band answer because it has good knowledge of changes. It could have been even better if there was some link to similar changes in a contrasting place beyond Powys. It was awarded 9 marks.

Applies AO2.1c to evaluate the relative impacts of change on rural settlements and their people.

The student does not really evaluate the changes, although a perceptive afterthought about it depends on the place or places being used as to which reasons are more important. It does mention people and places and gives the essay a context. It is a well-structured response. Perhaps more emphasis could have been placed on different places because these two are essentially the same. It is top-band 4 marks.

Knowledge check answers

1 The Lake District has been opened up by transport, initially the railway, but in Rebanks' time by the car and coach tours that can reach the area on the M6 motorway. Economically, it is the rise of leisure and tourism that enable farms that are no longer viable to be used as second homes, holiday cottages and for B&B accommodation. Traditional farming survives. Demographically, the population is older, the young having left the area. Politically, National Park status does provide safeguards for the landscape.

2 At a small scale some suburban areas are defined by the fact that they are gated, e.g. Ruxley Heights, Surrey. Wembley and Twickenham are defined by the stadia to those who do not live there. The media often uses objects when referring to a place, such as the Tyne bridges for Newcastle. Artworks, such as the Antony Gormley statues, *Another Place* on the beach at Crosby, or the *Angel of the North* at Gateshead, provide identity for a Liverpool suburb and the entrance to Gateshead respectively. The local currency, such as the Brixton £, can also be found in other Transition Towns such as Totnes, Stroud and Lewes. Bristol and Exeter also have a local currency.

3 The data suggests that globalisation of activities has had an impact on the functions and activities in cities and suburbs. Ownership and therefore control is coming from outside of the UK. The last two rows show how much clothing is under the control of one company and that restaurants are also managed from further afield.

4 See table below.

5 Utopian: the unrealistic aim for a place and its people to be in a state of perfection. In 1516, Thomas More outlined his view of a utopian city. Philanthropic industrialists in the nineteenth century, such as Rowntree, Salt and Owen, all attempted to create utopian settlements for their workers. Howard's Garden City movement attempted to harness both the benefits of urban and rural living in Letchworth. Harlow new town was a socialist attempt to plan a utopian settlement.

6 You do not have to use the towns identified here. Cities with a range of activities that are well-rewarded, such as York with its university and lower paid industrial heritage and low-paid tourism, are a case in point. Likewise, it is a range of activities that place Northampton in the same category. Coastal places such as Worthing, with an elderly population and a large care sector, will have low-paid employment together with higher paid tertiary employment. The percentage working in high-wage occupations is projected to grow. Low wage occupations are also growing and are predicted to exceed those in middle-wage occupations.

7 (a) Advantages: just shows the city and indicates numbers of jobs. A good initial impression of where employment is located.

(b) Disadvantages: areas other than centre and EZ are not named. There is no scale for the blocks, and there is no distance scale.

8 Approaching half of all electronics, books and music are purchased online. On the other hand, fashion goods and groceries together with electronics form 77% of sales by value. Overall it is the convenience of purchases from home, especially for those at work and for those unable to get to shops, that makes it preferable. Small items such as music

Group/ organisation	Engagement with harbour	How harbour locality is perceived	Experiences that influence perception of place
Local residents	Chose to live or have always lived in settlements	Under pressure	Extensions to existing villages, refurbished houses and second homes that increase the urban character of the settlements
Second-home owners	Chose to invest in property	Good place to visit with good amenities	Able to buy or even build a property; use of wealth to outbid local population; perceive it as a rural place, especially if resident in London or other major city
Yacht clubs	Year round; moorings, boat parks	Too many boats might spoil the water environment	Getting to water and onto it; quality of sailing environment
Parish Council	NIMBYism; want it to remain as it was in the past; large houses	Beauty, tranquillity, place of leisure; pressure on parking, waste disposal	Litter on shores; developers and redevelopment of existing properties
Conservancy	The environmental value of the waters — promotional; coastal protection	Home for wildlife, wintering grounds for birds	Bird watching
Farmers	Land has footpaths; fear of erosion from rising sea levels	Area into which land drains	Behaviour of walkers, litter

and books have fewer delivery problems and can be cheaper online. Grocery's rise is the value of digital convenience rather than locational convenience.

9 Much depends on the city or town (former warehouses and dockside buildings, former factories and workshops, former council-owned tower blocks, disused department stores, listed buildings that may include any of the above, areas of architecturally attractive housing located close to the city centre that had become rundown over time). It results in the city centre and some areas of the inner city having higher social status and the movement of low-income earners towards the suburbs. In the largest cities there may be a divide between the ultra-high wealth areas and other gentrified areas. Gentrification is altering the social geography so that the inner city and central city are housing more affluent groups, compared with the past when these areas were associated with lower income groups. Gentrification is occurring in many cities (Leeds, Liverpool, Newcastle, Cardiff). What types of buildings are being converted? What is the effect on the social geography of the city?

10 Peterborough has gained numbers employed in caring, elementary occupations and a few in management and the professions. The positive changes are similar in Stoke-on-Trent, although the rise in high-waged positions is greater. In both cities the intermediate-waged employees have declined by up to 20%. The trend is one in which both high-waged and low-waged sectors are growing, but it is the low-waged service sector that is increasing fastest. The changes from a manufacturing base to a service industry base are reflected in the graph.

11 Quick interpretation of graphs is an essential examination skill. The data is a mix of cities and regions and so is not always comparable. The data could be grouped into cities and regions. Also, the data does not give a baseline figure for any place. Many cities would have had a large number of companies in 2010.

The cities of the South are strongly represented, as are the capitals, but not Cardiff, which is subsumed into South Wales. There are some deindustrialised places, such as Liverpool, Greater Manchester, Hull and Sheffield, where companies have been able to start up. Research centres such as Oxford, Cambridge and Edinburgh have attracted digital companies.

12 The data is for the period 2008–12. It distinguishes rural, sparse rural and sparse (remote) rural. The fastest rise in jobs is in health education, but not in the more remote areas. Mining is in decline and agriculture has a small percentage increase. Overall, it is the rural and remote regions where there is growth and the less sparse areas where the number of jobs is in decline.

13 Remember, the data shows percentages in occupations. Therefore, the actual numbers might differ considerably, because more people live in urban areas. List where urban areas dominate, which are mainly in the lower waged areas. Rural areas have higher percentages of high-waged

persons as a result of counter-urbanisation together with a higher percentage of skilled trades (workers in agriculture and forestry need a variety of skills).

14 This question expects you to interpret opinions from the facts in the summary. A project cannot keep going if it is dependent on continuous external funding. Many of the attractions cater for a specifically narrow clientele, e.g. young adventure-seeking people. Some may suggest that there are more pressing issues to be addressed. The last bullet point hints at social and health problems. Allotments might be viewed favourably by the older generation as will smart energy, but access to services and transport to towns are not mentioned. Do the schemes retain the population or are the young leaving for university and higher paid employment?

15 The population living in rural areas is ageing; more are 60–74 and over 75 in 2011 compared with 2001. The number of children aged 0–14 has declined as has the number in the child-rearing age group, 30–44. These changes have implications for care and school places. Figure 38 only refers to the proportion in the working-age groups and early retirement. It is also about 'usual residents' and not second homes. Almost one-third is in the highest wage earning groups. Skilled trades are mainly agricultural, forestry and quarrying workers. Middle earners are almost half of the earners. The data supports the view that rural areas are very much regions of well-paid employment and relative affluence, although about 1 in 5 are among the low-paid persons. The impact of counter-urbanisation is evident. Issues are about impact on house prices, care and access to care, and second homes.

16 Benefits:
  (a) Space would provide accommodation for the young and those starting out
  (b) Space unoccupied in many cases
  (c) Brings more people into the city centre
  (d) Might suit particular groups for whom access to centre is difficult, e.g. non-drivers
  (e) Might be ideal for the excluded from society given supervision (by whom?)
  Costs:
  (a) Security unless there is separate access to upper floors
  (b) Who pays to bring space into use?
  (c) Could attract the excluded from society
  (d) Safety and fire regulation. Do the landowners want to cooperate?

17 Introductory sentence or two saying what you intend.
  (a) This is a simplistic view that suggests a split society both socially and spatially. At the basic level there is evidence that this occurs: Figure 44.
  (b) It is more complicated as there are gradations of areas based on age of population, age of buildings, tenure, economic activities. Explain with reference to your home place.
  (c) Conclude, summarising your main points. The question is evaluative so remember to say 'how far'.

Self-study task answers

Page 32   LQ calculation

$$LQ = \frac{\text{\% of the total workforce in an area working in an activity}}{\begin{array}{c}\text{the workforce in that activity in the country as a}\\\text{percentage of the total workforce}\end{array}}$$

Table 1 Number employed in skilled trades in UK statistical regions (2015)

UK statistical region	% working in skilled trades in region	% of skilled trades workers in UK workforce	LQ
South East	10.1	10.7	
London	8.0	10.7	0.74
South West	11.8	10.7	1.10
East	11.2	10.7	1.04
West Midlands	11.5	10.7	1.07
East Midlands	10.6	10.7	0.99
Yorks & Humber	11.6	10.7	1.08
North West	10.5	10.7	0.98
North East	11.4	10.7	1.06
Scotland	11.3	10.7	1.05
Northern Ireland	12.0	10.7	1.12
Wales	12.7	10.7	

Another way to illustrate an uneven distribution is to construct a **Lorenz curve**. Figure 1 shows the Lorenz curve constructed from data in Table 2, showing the regional share of Gross Value Added (GVA) per person in 2014.

Table 2 Regional share of GVA per person in 2014

UK region	GVA %	UK region	GVA %
London	22.6	Yorks & Humber	6.6
South East	14.9	East Midlands	5.9
North West	9.3	Wales	3.4
East	8.6	North East	3.0
Scotland	7.7	Northern Ireland	2.1
South West	7.5	Other areas	1.4
West Midlands	7.1		

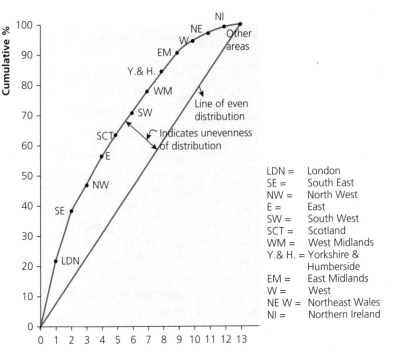

Figure 1 Lorenz curve for regional share of gross value added per person (2014)

The curve indicates that the distribution is uneven, otherwise it would fit the line of even distribution with the same proportion as the GVA per person in each region. It stresses the dominance of London and the South East as the regions with the greatest earnings, which then translates into other examples of affluence that affect people and their lives in those areas. At the opposite end of the scale, three peripheral regions have between 7 and 10 times less value added per person, which will inevitably affect lives.

Page 38 Self-study task: statistical 1

1 To calculate the **mean** use the formula below:

$$\frac{\Sigma x}{n} = \frac{297.7}{14}$$

where Σx is the sum of the figures and n is the number of data entries.
- Arithmetic mean is 21.26.
- Mode is 32.8.
- Median is 21.5 the middle value.

2 To calculate the **standard deviation** use the following formula:

$$\Sigma = \frac{\sqrt{(x-x)^2}}{n}$$

Deviation from the median: This is found by further dividing the values so that there are four equal parts, or quarters. Where the divide occurs is the quartile. In this data, the quartiles are 25.1 = Upper quartile and 16.8 = Lower quartile.

Page 38 Self-study task: statistical 2
- South East 0.94; Wales 1.18
- East Midlands has the nearest concentration to that of the UK.

  The concentrations are lower in the South East where the service economy is stronger. There are greater concentrations in the periphery, where modern economic activities have fewer employees.

Index

Index

Index